BUILD
YOUR
OWN
LADDER

| 4 | secrets
to making
your
career dreams
come true

DR. TONY ZEISS

NELSON BUSINESS
A Division of Thomas Nelson Publishers
Since 1798

www.thomasnelson.com

Published in Nashville, Tennessee, by Thomas Nelson, Inc.

Nelson Books titles may be purchased in bulk for educational, business, fundraising, or sales promotional use. For information, please e-mail SpecialMarkets@ThomasNelson.com.

Unless otherwise noted, Scripture quotations are from the NEW AMERICAN STANDARD BIBLE®, © Copyright The Lockman Foundation 1960, 1962, 1963, 1968, 1971, 1972, 1973, 1975, 1977. Used by permission. www.Lockman.org.

Scripture quotations noted KJV are from the KING JAMES VERSION of the Bible.

Library of Congress Cataloging-in-Publication Data

Zeiss, Anthony.
    Build your own ladder : four secrets to making your career dreams come true / Tony Zeiss.
        p. cm.
Includes bibliographical references.
    ISBN 0-7852-1260-4 (hardcover)
    1. Career development. 2. Success in business. I. Title.
    HF5381.Z332 2006
    650.14—dc22

                                                              2005028563

Printed in the United States of America

06 07 08 09 10 11 QW 1 2 3 4 5 6 7 8 9

I dedicate this book to all who aspire
to achieve productive and successful careers.

CONTENTS

INTRODUCTION

Are you living your dreams? Are you a success? Are you satisfied with your career? If not, do you have a plan to help you obtain your career goals? What steps will you take?

You can greatly improve your prospects of having a brilliantly successful career by doing what thousands of successful people have done before you.

The purpose of this book is to help you set a vision and develop the knowledge for achieving the career goals of your dreams. In effect, as you read and assimilate the information in this book, you will be designing and building your career ladder for success.

Most people spend more time working than in any other endeavor in life; yet they often leave their careers to chance. Although they have career dreams, they don't know how to achieve them. The principles in this book represent a collective body of knowledge and experience spanning from ancient to modern times.

Build Your Own Ladder will teach you the secrets that highly successful people have known for thousands of years. Successful people work from a personal vision, control their thinking, influence others, and employ the principle of reciprocity. They have achieved unparalleled success, and so can you!

This practical book will provide you the opportunity to develop your personal road map to career success and will teach you how to achieve significance through your work. At the end of each chapter you will find open-ended questions that, if you answer them honestly, will supply a basic business plan that works for you.

The first chapter introduces you to today's world of work and presents a basic overview of what it takes to be successful in a career. Chapter 2 helps you set the career vision of your dreams. Chapter 3 focuses on the power of disciplining your thoughts and forming healthy, positive beliefs about your life, and chapter 4 provides insight on the mind-body connection. Chapter 5 examines the importance of being influential and teaches you how to expand your influence at the workplace. Chapter 6 discusses the principle of reciprocity and how it can give you the clear edge over any barrier or competitor. Chapter 7 identifies the key principles of leadership and offers wonderful career-building advice from others who have already succeeded in achieving outstanding careers.

This is an unusual book. If you read it, think about it, and employ the wisdom of the ages compiled in the narrative, you will arm yourself for complete success. By learning and practicing these principles, you will exceed your current expectations and have an extraordinary career. As you achieve your career success, I request only that you share this knowledge for personal success with others.

| 1 |

PREPARE FOR UNENDING CAREER SUCCESS

Failure to prepare is preparing to fail.
—Anonymous

THE CURRENT WORLD OF WORK

There has never been a better time to establish the career of your dreams!

America is in the beginning stages of the greatest labor and skills shortage of its history. Labor economists predict that we will experience a shortage of more than 10 million workers by 2011.[1] Further, a serious lack of skilled workers in all careers began in 2005 and will extend to an estimated shortage of 21 million workers by 2020. The shortages will be most acute among those in management and high-technology careers.[2] Baby boomers are retiring by the hundreds of thousands, and employers are eager to replace them with skilled workers.

Technological advances are opening entirely new career options no one dreamed of even a few years ago. Bioinformatics, geospatial technology, hydrogen fuel cell technology, and similar high-tech career options are providing broader career options for today's workers. These are most exciting times for emerging workers who wish to establish personal career plans and for those who are already in the workforce and wish to navigate these workplace changes successfully.

The U.S. Department of Labor publishes a list of the fastest-growing occupations that may be of interest as you consider your career goal. They primarily include health care, automotive technology, construction, and computer software professions. There are emerging occupations in technology, and the demand for teachers and security professionals is growing rapidly. You can access this information at http://www.bls.gov/emp/emptab3.htm. If you are a young person, I urge you to talk with your parents and older people about how to advance in a career, but don't expect them to help you choose a high-tech career field. Most of these jobs weren't around even five years ago.

With few exceptions, today's workers are outlasting the lives of their companies. The days of dedicating one's total working life to one organization are generally gone. Today's workers will likely work forty-five years, change jobs seven or more times, and change career fields three or four times. Smart people are preparing themselves with the knowledge and skills to be competitive in the marketplace today and in the future. They see learning as a lifelong endeavor, and they keep pace with changing technology and changing businesses. In effect, they see themselves as individual enterprises. When one customer (employer) no longer needs their services, they shop for another one.

> Today's workers will likely work forty-five years, change jobs seven or more times, and change career fields three or four times.

You do not exist just to make money! A career should be fun and provide meaning to your life. If your current career doesn't supply these things, it's time to change careers. If you are just now entering the workforce, resolve to think this way from the beginning. There are plenty of exciting opportunities for anyone who has the ability to set a career vision, develop a plan, and work the plan.

Think about it. Your career options are almost innumerable if you prepare yourself with the knowledge and skills necessary to compete in the marketplace. Your chances for achieving a pinnacle experience in your career will be much improved if you also learn to harness the power of vision and thought, learn to be influential, and use the principle of reciprocity.

The choice is up to you. The human potential is awesome. Excepting certain physical limitations, you can become anything you choose and believe you can become. You may be thinking you are too old to start over. This is nonsense. Colonel Sanders of Kentucky Fried Chicken fame was in his late sixties when he began that business. Grandma Moses achieved artistic fame in her seventies. As President of Central Piedmont Community College in Charlotte, North Carolina, I was privileged to award a ninety-year-young great-grandmother her high school diploma last year. These people refused to limit themselves.

You may also be thinking that you're too young to be what you really want to be. Consider Michael Dell or Bill Gates, or Larry Page and Sergey Brin, the two Stanford University graduate students who invented Google. Knowledge is more important than age. Besides, you won't always be young. The question is whether you will grow older in the career you want, or just grow older.

> Knowledge is more important than age. Besides, you won't always be young. The question is whether you will grow older in the career you want, or just grow older.

Perhaps you think that you don't have the intelligence to attain the career of your dreams because your college entrance scores were low or you didn't do well in school. Guess what? The greatest predictor of career success is not your IQ or the grades you made in high school. *I have been in education for thirty-five years, and I can verify that the most reliable predictor of career success is the ability to set a personal career vision and be willing to work toward achieving it.*

It is time to seize the day! The time to expand your vision, drop the thoughts that limit your growth, and claim the career of your dreams is now, this moment. Let's get started with a plan that will work for you. But first you must understand what it is all about. After all, you will spend most of your life working, and it is vital to give some serious thought about your options, your career goal, and the development of a plan for ensuring success.

A ROAD MAP FOR CAREER SUCCESS

At age seventeen I determined to become a teacher. At age twenty-two I set the goal of becoming a college president. When I turned twenty-six, I decided to also become a significant writer and speaker about education and workforce development. I was fortunate that my father taught me how to set goals and pursue them. I have achieved these major career goals because I first learned to set them.

TRY TO BECOME LIKE THOSE YOU MOST ADMIRE

I recommend that you try to find a mentor, preferably someone who is accomplished in your chosen career field, to give you the benefit of his or her experience. If you can't find a mentor, look for people whom you admire in your career field, and observe them whenever possible. You will be surprised what you can learn. My first mentor was Dr. Isaac Beckes, president of Vincennes University back in the early seventies. He did not know he was my mentor, but I came to admire him so much that he became a vicarious mentor. I observed how he handled people and how he dealt with challenges, and I still emulate some of his behaviors today.

In my thirty-five-year career I have taught at the high school level, at the community college level, and at the university level. I have enjoyed a wonderful career, especially for the past twenty years as a community college president. I am currently privileged to lead Central Piedmont Community College in Charlotte, North Carolina. This fine college serves more than seventy thousand students each year through six campuses and a large online operation. When I was twenty-two years old I set the goal to become a community college president by age forty-four. I wanted to make a difference in the lives of people, just as Dr. Beckes was doing. It was an ambitious goal for a young man who was the first in his family of eight children to attend college and who supported himself financially. But I was able to overcome the doubts and fears that plagued me, and I set the goal. From that point forward, I thought of myself as one who was becoming a community college president.

Since that time, I have been an observer of people and their careers, and I have contributed to the research regarding workforce and career development. The collective knowledge from years of research in the field and the experience of helping hundreds of people mold stellar careers have helped me develop a guaranteed career-success formula. Setting the career goal is the major first step, but you have to have a plan as your road map for success.

> The collective knowledge from years of research in the field and the experience of helping hundreds of people mold stellar careers have helped me develop a guaranteed career-success formula.

This formula will work for people who employ it and customize it for themselves.

Those who achieve their highest dreams of career success learn to use the following:

1. The power of vision
2. The power of thought
3. The power of influence
4. The power of reciprocity

Each of these concepts will be thoroughly addressed in the succeeding chapters. Before any of these career-enhancing properties can be useful, however, you must have the physical capability and the burning desire to succeed.

BE PHYSICALLY FIT

If you take care of your body, your body will take care of you. If you abuse your body, it will become a liability as you attempt to achieve career success. We all know how important our automobiles have become. We generally can't get to work without them. We've learned to take care of our automobiles by keeping them well serviced. The same is true of our bodies. If we don't maintain them well, they won't be able to serve us well.

Working in a career for an average of forty-five years requires physical stamina. Don't choose a career that is a mismatch for your body. If you would love to play professional football, but weigh 120 pounds, you might consider a different career you could love. To achieve greatness in a career, you generally must work at it for two or three decades. Your body has to be able to get you through those years with a minimum of problems. You know that a healthy diet and exercise are essential to your well-being. If you hope to be a giant in your career, a good diet and regular exercise must become part of your life's balance.

People Treat You As They See You

Your appearance can be your best asset or your worst liability as you climb up the career ladder. First impressions are critical, and you will always be making first impressions. Early in my career, I couldn't afford a large wardrobe, but I made sure my clothes were clean and well pressed, and I kept my body trim and my hair combed. My wife gave me a book on dressing for success and encouraged me to smile more often. It was difficult for me to smile since my teeth were crooked, and I was painfully aware of that imperfection. I smiled anyway, and it helped. At forty years of age, I finally had the money and the courage to get braces, and my smile got even broader!

People treat you as they perceive you. This is a simple fact of life. Teenagers are often heard to exclaim that someone has judged them unfairly because of their outlandish dress, hairdos, or body piercing. If someone is screaming for attention through his appearance, how could the observer not draw a conclusion that he is insecure? People the world over process information and draw conclusions about others by their appearance and their behavior. This is human nature, which has not changed through-out history and will likely never change much. Everyone looks at himself in the mirror before going for a job interview, but successful career seekers assess their appearance before going to work each day. They understand the importance of packaging.

Your dress, hygiene, breath, posture, grooming, body language, facial expressions, and speech contribute to your ability to make and keep good impressions. A smart professional displays an attitude of alertness, vitality, and confidence on a consistent basis, including informal times when people observe you without your knowledge. You will be wise to pay attention to the dress and behavior of the leaders in your company and your career field. The accepted or expected dress and behavior of leaders in your career field are part of the culture of the organization and usually the profession. The more your dress and behavior conform to the established culture, the more likely you will be viewed favorably.

HAVE A BURNING DESIRE

If necessity is the mother of invention, desire is the mother of action. We can dream of happiness, fame, and prosperity, but if we don't take action to achieve these things, it is only a dream. Almost all people have dreams of great careers, but relatively few actually reach them. Why? They fail to plan for that great career, or they fail to execute their plan. They allow circumstances to serve as their excuse. The most common excuses include lack of time, being too busy with children, and not having enough resources to seek and obtain the needed training or degree. All of these excuses can be plausible at times, but not all of the time. The root of the problem is the lack of desire.

One of my favorite student success stories involves a young, single father of two who had a burning desire to begin a career in the graphic arts field. He had the odds stacked against him. Kevin and his children were living with his mother, a ninety-minute drive from our college. He worked part-time, but still could hardly make ends meet. He had plenty of good reasons for not even starting on a career path. Nevertheless, Kevin felt that burning desire to prepare for a career in his chosen field. He applied for and received federal financial aid and enrolled in classes. He drove his very-used car to school every weekday for two years. It was his desire that drove him to succeed. He was simply too busy winning to lose. Not surprisingly, Kevin earned his degree and is working with one of Charlotte's largest employers.

I could share a thousand similar stories with you, and the results are always the same. The person with the *vision* and the *desire* to succeed will succeed. If desire could be packaged and sold, the whole world would be a better place.

Unfortunately, some people have the desire, but it fades into obscurity because they lack the motivation to execute it. They do not put their career plans into action.

No one can really motivate anyone else. All that can be done is to convince someone that he has the power to become anything he wants if he wants to badly enough. People can be encouraged to take action, but in the end the choice is theirs and theirs alone. The root of self-motivation lies in what people value and in what they believe.

If you value the idea of owning a beautiful home on the beach, but don't believe you could ever afford such a luxury, you will never own a home on the beach. By the same token, if you believe you could someday own a Harley-Davidson motorcycle, but you see no value in owning such a vehicle, you won't purchase one. If you don't value a certain career field, if it doesn't excite you, strike it off your list of possible careers. You can't fake your way to career success, and even if you could, do you want to spend forty-five years doing something you don't like? On the other hand, you can change your beliefs or expectations about your ability to succeed at one thing or another.

> If you don't value a certain career field, if it doesn't excite you, strike it off your list of possible careers. You can't fake your way to career success, and even if you could, do you want to spend forty-five years doing something you don't like?

Therefore, if you have a dream career for which you have the physical capacity, but doubt your ability to achieve it, be of good cheer! You can overcome your doubts and insecurities by learning to believe in yourself. We will explore this topic and provide you with the techniques for increasing your vision and expectations in chapters 2 and 3. Meanwhile, it is valuable to understand how most people progress through their careers.

Essentially people take more risks in their careers and raise their career goals as they gain confidence in their abilities. As you progress through your career and gain confidence, your insecurities melt away naturally. Most people begin at entry-level jobs and progress up the ladder. As they learn on the job and are successful, they are more willing to work for the next promotion. This is a natural process for most people, but it is often very time-consuming, and many people never reach their full potential. You can learn to circumvent this process by setting a higher career goal from the beginning. If your plan is to become the CEO, you will be following a time plan for reaching that goal, always working with a purpose to move up the ladder.

Years ago an author wrote about his theory that people in the workplace eventually rise above their level of competence. This may be the case in some circumstances, but it is far from the norm. My experience has been that most people limit themselves from ever reaching their career potential. They convince themselves that they are happy where they are and have no desire to rise farther. In reality, they are usually afraid of failure or have some other insecurity that prevents them from risking another career move. They either forgot or never learned that the capacity of ordinary humans to achieve extraordinary success lies within themselves. Don't shortchange your life. Aim high, because we usually hit what we aim at!

KNOWLEDGE IS POWER

To be successful in any career, you must be proficient in three areas:

1. Academic ability
2. Technical aptitude
3. Social skills

Professionals Are Knowledgeable

Every career in America today requires a mastery of the basic skills of reading, writing, and computation. If you haven't mastered these fundamental literacy skills, the first goal in your career plan is to eliminate your deficiencies. To get started in a decent career with growth potential, you must have mastered these basic skills at least at the tenth-grade level, and you must hold a high school diploma or the equivalent. You must also be proficient in the new basic skills that include information-gathering via the Internet, analytical skills, the ability to communicate and work well with others, and computer keyboard skills.

If you are not proficient in each of these areas, I encourage you to take a positive step toward a better future by enrolling at your local community college. College entrance counselors can assess your academic preparedness and prescribe a program that will help you overcome any deficiencies. Employers across the country are concerned about employees with low basic skills.

One of the most courageous people I have ever known was an illiterate sixty-four-year-old man whose goal was to learn to read and write. He enrolled in a workplace literacy course we provided at his place of employment some years ago. After three months of training and with tears of pride streaming down his face, he told those who attended the course completion ceremony that he had just achieved a lifelong goal by writing personal notes on every Christmas card he sent to his family and friends. Don't be afraid to learn; be afraid not to.

All Jobs Require Technical Proficiency

If you already know the career you want to pursue, place yourself in a position to get the specific technical training needed to be employed or promoted. Once you master the occupational skills for the entry level, you should begin training to acquire the skills needed for the next job on your career ladder. If you are not sure about the specific technical skills you will need for your career, talk to people in the field, look it up through the North American Industry Classification System's Web site at www.census.gov/naics, see a career counselor at a college, or find the information at a public library. Learning has become a lifelong necessity, and those willing to continue growing in knowledge and technical skills will continue growing in their careers.

> Don't be afraid to learn; be afraid not to.

If time and/or money are barriers to your continued education, visit a college career counselor as soon as possible, and explain your challenges. Most colleges have abundant financial aid opportunities and also provide education and training at convenient times for working adults. And don't worry about how long you may have been out of school. These colleges are filled with people of all ages.

Social Skills Are Most Critical for Career Success

In addition to the basic academic and field-specific technical skills, you will need to develop your social skills to their optimum. The abilities to communicate effectively, work with others, and be customer focused are essential for career success. If you can't compose clear e-mails or write well, your career will be in jeopardy. If you have poor interpersonal communication skills in small groups, one to one, or via the telephone, your career growth will be stunted. If you cannot make effective presentations, you will likely never be given the opportunity to become a senior officer. If you can't get along with others or let others take credit for good work, you will be frozen in your progress. Finally, you must understand that being customer focused is a

> Being customer focused is a requirement for anyone who hopes to progress in his or her career. By the way, everyone is your customer.

requirement for anyone who hopes to progress in his or her career. By the way, everyone is your customer.

The bottom line here is to take an honest assessment of your knowledge and technical skills related to your career plan and act to correct any deficiencies. More than that, you should learn more than you need for your current job, always positioning yourself for the next level of responsibility. You must also learn to use the social skills that build trusting relationships. Keep your eye on the prize, and keep learning to earn the next promotion.

My research on the attributes most desired by employers underscores the importance of these social or attitudinal skills in employees.[3]

Here are the desired employee characteristics most appreciated by American employers in priority order:

1. They are positive in their attitudes.
2. They are good communicators.
3. They are dependable and responsible.
4. They are good team workers.
5. They are good problem solvers.

6. They are service oriented.
7. They are results oriented.
8. They are organized.
9. They are influential.
10. They are learning oriented.
11. They are academically and technically skilled.
12. They are experienced.

Please note that the first ten characteristics preferred by employers are attitudinal in nature. Each one is within everyone's ability to practice. If you want to move up the career ladder or increase your company's business, practice these things.

TO ENSURE CAREER SUCCESS

My hope is that this chapter has whetted your appetite to learn more about the techniques of gaining the career of your dreams. You will achieve anything in your career if you develop and maintain the motivation and burning desire to achieve it. Believe me; you will astound yourself and those around you if you follow the advice in this book. The more you understand and employ the powers of vision, thought, influence, and reciprocity, the more successful you will become.

Choosing, developing, and managing careers are adventures to those who love to be able to make a difference in others. Every occupation, whether you work for others or yourself, will afford you the opportunity to make a difference. I love my work, and it is my hope that you will be able to choose and have a career that brings you as much happiness. You're about to embark on a wonderful career adventure, and the biggest step is the first one: learning how to choose a personal career vision. Chapter 2 is dedicated to this end.

| LADDER-BUILDING TIPS |

1. Recognize that you are living in a great time for developing a great career.
2. Only you can choose your career goal and develop a plan for achieving it.
3. The powers of vision, thought, influence, and reciprocity will guide you to success.
4. Personal desire and motivation must provide the fuel for career success.
5. Begin with a solid foundation of the basic academic, technical, and social skills.
6. Academic and technical skills are essential for good careers, but it's the social skills that make good careers great careers!

| LADDER-BUILDING ACTIONS |

Note: This section will appear at the end of each chapter, and it is designed to help you contemplate and internalize your thoughts about your career path. The accumulation of all of your answers to these affirmations will provide the basis for your personal road map for career success.

From this day forward:

1. I will (for example) *recognize that I can become anything I wish if I have the desire and motivation to act on it.*
From this day forward, I will:

_____

_____

_____

2. I resolve (for example) *to examine my career options and set a personal career vision within the next thirty days.*
   From this day forward, I resolve:

_____

_____

_____

3. I resolve (for example) *to finish reading this book!*
   I resolve:

_____

_____

_____

| 2 |

THE POWER OF VISION

Awaken the Genius Within You

Whether you think you can or you
think you can't, you're right.
—Henry Ford

DEVELOP A SENSE OF SELF

Who are you? What do you wish to become? No one can answer these questions but you. I mentioned that I answered these questions at age twenty-two by determining that I was most of all a teacher and that I would become a community college president by age forty-four. NASCAR great Jeff Gordon didn't suddenly become a famous race car legend. He understood who he was and that he could be as good as or better than any other drivers. He also set a goal to be a NASCAR driver at a very early age. My good friend Rick Hendrick of Hendrick Motorsports determined early on that he would make his living in the automobile business and try to become the best at it in the country. No successful people are handed their success. They are just ordinary people who set extraordinary goals for themselves and had the passion to work toward them.

You have been designed for success, even greatness. Have you defined what that success is for you? If you haven't clearly defined it, how will you ever achieve it?

The point is obvious. We can't achieve something unless it has first been conceived and defined. Vision always precedes success. There is tremendous power in having a vision. The Good Book says, "Where there is no vision, the people perish."[1] Nations without a vision suffer and are overthrown. Organizations without clear visions disappear. Saddest of all are people who have no personal vision and waste their lives.

Many professional educators used to think that the most accurate predictor of career success was your intelligence quotient, or IQ. In retrospect, I am glad they never told us what our IQs were back in high school. We would have labeled ourselves as our teachers labeled us. I never knew if I was dumb or smart! In the middle 1960s I once had a college professor assign grades based on our SAT scores rather than what we earned through our examinations in his class. Neither your IQ, nor any other test for intelligence, nor acquired knowledge is a good predictor of your future career success.

> Neither your IQ, nor any other test for intelligence, nor acquired knowledge is a good predictor of your future career success.

In the 1970s many educators and psychologists believed that your socioeconomic condition was the best predictor of career success. Others thought your accumulated grade point average could predict career success. All of them were wrong. The greatest predictor of career success is your ability to set a career vision, believe you can achieve it, and work hard at your plan to accomplish it. Your passion and desire to reach your career goal will help you realize it more than all the tests or good grades put together. Setting a personal vision for career success is critical for your future destiny.

It has often been said that knowing the objective is half the battle, and so it is with your career. Once you have set a vision for your dream career, it is easier to get and stay focused on that objective. Almost magically your conscious and subconscious thoughts will guide you toward achieving the goal as though it were a magnet. Before examining how to set a personal career vision, you would do well to look into the business of self-discovery. If you don't really know yourself and understand that your limitations are largely self-imposed, you cannot easily set a personal vision that will keep you motivated to achieve it.

The ability to shape life to our liking is a remarkable gift. This gift also demands that we take the responsibility for it. God has given each of us the ability to set a course for our lives and to adopt a set of values by which we will conduct ourselves. Pierre Teilhard de Chardin said, "We are not human beings having a spiritual experience. We are spiritual beings having a human experience." So let's make the best of this experience by learning how to focus and achieve the career vision of a lifetime.

We are accountable for how we live, behave, and grow as human beings. There are undeniable spiritual or universal laws that affect us, just as there are physical laws under which we live. If we cheat or lie our way into a promotion, we will be found out. If we violate a personal value, our consciences will bother us until we right the wrong. As we go through the process of life, we are establishing a belief system that affects all that we do. We are in a perpetual state of learning what works for us and what doesn't. We gravitate toward the things that reinforce our beliefs, and we do more of the things that work for us. Once we understand this process and establish our beliefs and personal values, we increasingly discover a clear sense of who we are.

Our sense of self comes from our thoughts, values, and beliefs that have been forged by the external and internal stimuli to which we have been exposed. This sense of self directs our thinking about ourselves and our relationship to the world. If you don't really believe you could become a heart surgeon, you won't even consider becoming one. If the inner voice within you suggests that you won't be successful at an endeavor, you won't attempt it. Since one purpose of this book is to help you set an extraordinary vision for your career, you first have to understand how your sense of self has been developed. Once you understand how it has been developed, you can begin to direct your thoughts and experiences to broaden it if need be.

Futurist Joel Barker, in his video presentation *The Power of Vision,* explains that "once we understand how our paradigms influence our perceptions of the world around us, we begin to see why we miss important data that will shape the future. And once we realize that, we can begin to actively correct that blindness."[2] Paradigms refer to the way we perceive the world, our beliefs, and concepts of reality.

As we develop through childhood and into adulthood, our sense of self is created. We establish a set of moral and social values by observing our parents and other significant people, including church leaders and teachers. Their influence is especially important in the development of our sense of self. If a significant person in your life, such as a parent, an aunt, or a teacher, suggests that you are not as attractive as your siblings, you will believe it. If a math teacher suggests that you are a poor math student, you will believe that also. On the other hand, if a subsequent math teacher suggests that you are a natural at understanding mathematical concepts, you will work hard to live up to those expectations, thereby improving your ability to do math and your self-esteem. If you attempt to play basketball and become an expert at bench warming and you have a similar experience at volleyball, you will likely conclude that you are not a good athlete. However, you may later find that you can play golf with the best of them, causing you to change your belief about your athleticism. These positive and negative social experiences shape us into what we think of ourselves.

Our self-esteem has a huge effect on what we will attempt to do. If we don't believe we can dance, for example, we will not attempt to dance for fear of embarrassing ourselves. And each time we refuse to dance, we reinforce the belief that we can't dance. On the other hand, we have all seen plenty of people whom we judge to be terrible dancers, but they believe they are good dancers. Those who dance poorly get just as much gratification from their dancing as do those who dance well. What we believe is the only thing that really affects whether we dance or not.

The good news is that we can put ourselves into circumstances that can change the way we think about ourselves. People don't like to take risks that may diminish their self-esteem, especially if they have no confidence in achieving a certain thing. But by consciously taking very small risks, you can change your belief about your ability. If you think you are a poor speaker but would like to be a good speaker, take a class. If that is too frightening, volunteer to teach a Sunday school class or be a substitute for one. Force yourself to begin speaking in front of others even on a very casual basis. Practice speaking while facing a mirror. Join a Toastmasters club. Do whatever it takes to replace your lack of confidence with increased confidence as a speaker. As you improve your speaking ability, the positive feedback you receive from your audiences will also boost your confidence. Over time and with practice, you will become a good public speaker, and your inner belief about your ability as a speaker will change. Positive people place themselves in circumstances for improvement.

Psychologists tell us that human motivation in its simplest form is nothing more than a system of rewards and punishments. B. F. Skinner emphasized this basic premise by developing a theory for human motivation that is sometimes referred to as "reward psychology" or "behaviorism." The principal idea is that behavior that is rewarded will be repeated, and behavior that is ignored, or sometimes punished, will disappear. As we mature, we learn to use this principle to help ourselves.

As a young teacher, I wanted to improve my writing skills. Writing term papers had always been a chore, yet I admired those who could write well, and I knew that learning to write was an integral skill for my career. I decided that the best way to learn to write was by writing, so I volunteered to be the public relations liaison for our local Boy Scout Council. I labored mightily over the first few articles I submitted to the newspaper but saw very little actually published. Fortunately, a kind editor gave me some tips that helped. He even marked up one story in red ink so I could better understand how he wanted things written. I stuck with it, and within six months I was writing a weekly outdoor column.

I wrote newspaper columns and magazine articles for almost ten years and was rewarded every time I saw my writing in print and every time someone mentioned reading my work. This is the eighteenth or nineteenth book I have authored or coauthored. Placing yourself in positions to improve an aspect of your life is uncomfortable in the beginning, but the rewards are well worth the effort. Remember, I did not begin by writing a book. I began by writing a newspaper story about Scouting, and I was grateful for constructive criticism.

IT'S OKAY TO CHANGE YOUR MIND

Some people feel a "calling" to one career or another. Some church friends of ours gave up their first careers of business and teaching to respond to their calling to be missionaries to children in Mexico. They knew nothing about being missionaries, but they felt compelled to learn. They volunteered to intern with some missionaries who directed an orphanage and a school in central Mexico. Now, four years later, our friends are in Cozumel, Mexico, where they have established an orphanage and school of their own and are enjoying their new dream careers. I hope you can set such a compelling career vision. If you can, you are well on your way to outstanding career success!

Dr. Seuss probably summed up the idea as well as anyone in his landmark children's book *Oh, the Places You'll Go!* "You have brains in your head. You have feet in your shoes. You can steer yourself any direction you choose. You're on your own, and you know what you know. And YOU are the guy who'll decide where to go."[3]

We can alter our course anytime we choose. We can also learn to gain the confidence we need in order to establish and achieve grand visions for ourselves. We gain confidence by taking small risks to begin with, then building upon small successes until we can take bigger risks and receive bigger successes. Success really does breed success. In this way, we are always growing, expanding our horizons, and achieving new heights. This is what life and careers are about. On the contrary, if we think we have arrived at the peak of our career or are unwilling to take new risks or new challenges, we stagnate and waste the potential for doing greater good for others and achieving greater personal fulfillment. I tell my staff that the moment they begin to feel comfortable in their jobs, they should be looking for one within the college that has a higher challenge. I believe humans must be in a perpetual state of self-improvement.

You were born with the ability to make a difference. You have the capacity to make a difference in your world and in those whom you influence. The choice is up to you. Will you use your gifts to reach your full potential in your career, or will you play it safe? If you play it safe and limit your potential, you will literally miss the opportunities of a lifetime. If you do not develop and share your latent talents, you will have missed the best part of life.

> Will you use your gifts to reach your full potential in your career, or will you play it safe? If you play it safe and limit your potential, you will literally miss the opportunities of a lifetime. If you do not develop and share your latent talents, you will have missed the best part of life.

Only fear or self-doubt can keep you from choosing the career vision you would really like to choose. Once you understand that those fears and doubts were created through early negative social experiences and sometimes from later significant emotional experiences, you can take positive steps to eliminate them. Remember, fears and doubts aren't tangible; they are simply manifestations of your thoughts. Confront them; work through them mentally, not emotionally; and dismiss them. To ignore them is to allow them to continue limiting your true and full potential.

THERE IS POWER IN VISION

Our vision determines our destiny. Viktor Frankl, a Jewish psychiatrist from Vienna, was rounded up at the beginning of World War II and put in the Auschwitz concentration camp. He set a vision for himself, and he credits it with saving his life while thousands of other people died. He visualized himself lecturing in a large auditorium about his observations of human behavior in the concentration camp. He was determined to survive, help others as he could, and learn from the experience. Frankl did survive and became a renowned lecturer on the subject of the Holocaust. His book, *Man's Search for Meaning,* describes his observations and conclusions. His key observations are most instructive.

Frankl stated that those without a purpose, a reason to live for the future, perished. That ancient proverb about the importance of having a vision was verified at Auschwitz. Those who gave up hope, died. He also observed that men without a future goal declined mentally and physically by thinking retrospective thoughts, not future thoughts. Life for them became meaningless, and they died. From this experience Frankl launched a new psychological theory he named Logotherapy, literally translating to "therapy through meaning." Essentially he purported that man's main concern is not to gain pleasure or avoid pain, but to discover meaning in life. Without meaning, there is no hope. Without hope, men lost their health and expired.[4]

As I mentioned earlier, futurist Joel Barker prepared an outstanding video presentation that featured the power of vision. In this video, which I highly recommend, he proves unequivocally that "the power of vision shows that, at all human scales from nations to individuals, having a positive vision of the future is profoundly empowering."[5] Establishing a personal vision is certainly one of the most important things each of us does in this life. We must be serious about it because we must be true to ourselves.

Have you determined your life's purpose yet? What is it that you want to accomplish during your life? What kind of mark do you want to leave in this world? What kind of person do you want to become? Once you have answered these questions, you can more easily set a career vision. Your career should complement your purpose in life; otherwise, your work will be in constant conflict with what you really desire to become. I had a great automotive technology teacher who suddenly decided that, although he enjoyed teaching automotive mechanics, he really wanted to preach. He followed his new passion and enrolled in divinity school. I admired him for being true to his dream of making a spiritual difference for others. He simply decided to direct his career more in tune with his life's purpose.

My friend Allen Simonini was a biology major in college, but upon graduation, he decided what he really enjoyed was creating things that pleased people. Instead of using his biology degree, he followed his heart and chose to become a home builder. His company, Simonini Builders, is now one of the top custom home builders in the nation.

I once had an outstanding administrative assistant who, after twenty years, began to feel unfulfilled. What she really wanted to do was to please others and have her own business. She retired early and opened a gift shop. Last time I saw her, she was happy as a clam.

What causes people to change direction in careers? Usually they discover that their careers are incongruent with their purpose in life. They realize that they are not chained to one job or one career, that they can change direction, and that they can follow their life's passion by choosing to do so. These liberating moments are among the happiest in people's lives. If you have established your purpose in life, are you accomplishing it? Are you following your passion in the career you have chosen? No one can answer these penetrating questions but you.

Other people are successful in choosing a great career from the beginning. Two of my first college students demonstrated the power of vision. Gary was an excellent student and always presented himself well. John made good grades in subjects he liked, but not so good grades where his interests waned. He usually wore blue jeans with holes in the knees, and his hair was the longest in the class. One day I asked the students in my television production class to tell me their career goals. I received the usual vague answers, except from Gary and John. Both students had a clear vision for what they wanted to become.

Gary replied that he intended to become a network announcer for motor sports. John said that he intended to become a rock star. I was thrilled to later learn that both achieved their dream careers. Gary became Gary Lee of ESPN motor sports, and you know John as John Cougar Mellencamp, a highly successful rock-and-roll artist. In spite of their differences, both young men had visualized what they intended to become, and they stuck to their goals. They saw themselves as being in the process of becoming a network sportscaster and a rock star at the age of eighteen. In the end, it wasn't their academic experience that propelled Gary and John to success; it was their personal visions and the willingness to work toward achieving them that made the difference. When you set a career goal, you must see yourself as being in the process of becoming what you want. You must believe you will achieve it and be willing to work for it. You become what you believe yourself to be!

A friend of mine reminded me that life is not a dress rehearsal. This realization should motivate you to aim high when you are choosing a career goal. Gary and John aimed high and followed their passion. You should do the same thing.

Build a Tall Career Ladder

A vision should stretch your talent and expertise. In 1994 we set a vision for Central Piedmont Community College to be the nation's leader in workforce development. The college has recently been named the Community College of the Year by the National Alliance of Business and has been cited numerous times by independent studies as one of the top two colleges in the country in workforce development. Believe me, this vision for our college was a stretch in the mid-1990s, but the governing board and I never doubted we could achieve it. The key to success, however, was to see that the faculty and staff embraced the vision and believed it could be accomplished.

If your vision doesn't require substantial growth in knowledge and skills, it is not a vision worthy of your best efforts. Don't worry if the vision seems almost impossible. You will grow into it. Do you know more today than ten years ago? Do you have more skills today than ten years ago? Your knowledge and skills will continue to increase throughout your lifetime. No one has all the knowledge and skills necessary for achieving his top career position when he first begins.

I believe the power of vision is strongest when our purpose, our careers, and our daily lives are harmonious and work together for the same goal. Jesus has said that the two greatest commandments are to love God and to love others. The most successful people I know try to follow these commandments in their lives and through their work. Their purpose for living is driven by these commandments, and their values, beliefs, and passion emanate from this focused purpose. The secret to setting a career goal that will provide you the optimum chances for success is to choose one that is in harmony with your inner being and your purpose.

Ken Blanchard and Jesse Stoner, in a recent book titled *Full Steam Ahead! Unleash the Power of Vision in Your Company and Your Life,* explain that there are three key elements to a compelling vision: (1) significant purpose, (2) clear values, and (3) a picture of the future.[6] Simply stated, we must have an ever-present purpose, connect appropriate values to our lives, and visualize the future we really want.

Do you have a calling? Most people, when pressed, will tell you that they feel compelled to do one type of work or another. I have always felt called to be in education. I have other interests, of course, but my fundamental calling or purpose is to make a difference in others through my efforts in education. My career and my values are harmonious with my life's purpose. This creates a healthy balance in life that allows me to more easily accomplish the goals I have chosen.

SETTING YOUR VISION

An effective technique for selecting your dream career is to honestly answer the following questions in writing:

1. What is my overall purpose in this life?
2. What primary values will I choose to live by?
3. What would be the ideal career for me?
4. What ultimate position do I want to hold in my career?

Answering these questions may take some time. Don't be concerned with making quick decisions about your life. Spend some quality time alone in a quiet place. Listen to your inner self. Pray about these questions, and one by one you will find the answers. Remember to answer them in priority order. Questions 2, 3, and 4 should follow the first question. Your purpose and values will define you throughout your life. But you can change jobs and careers whenever you feel passionate about doing so, as long as the new job or career is harmonious with your purpose and values.

I cannot help you answer the first two questions, but I can help you determine the career you might want to consider, and I can give you a formula for career success. First, you have to know what you're good at!

DISCOVER YOUR UNIQUE ABILITY

Most people spend more time planning a family reunion or a Fourth of July picnic than planning their careers. Yet these same people are interested in having careers that are best suited to them. You can take most of the guesswork out of choosing your career by planning for it well. Dan Sullivan, president of The Strategic Coach, Inc., has achieved phenomenal career success by helping others achieve career success. He helps people discover their unique abilities, which he describes as a set of habits and talents that are unique to them. Have you determined your unique abilities?

> Most people spend more time planning a family reunion or a Fourth of July picnic than planning their careers. Yet these same people are interested in having careers that are best suited to them.

Robert Collier wrote a wonderful book back in the 1940s titled *Riches Within Your Reach: The Law of the Higher Potential.* In it he emphasized that there is something each of us can do better than anyone else, and the opportunities are plentiful. He stated, "All we need is a receptive mind, a willingness to try, and a persistence to see things through." He also said that in every person there is a "seed of life with infinite power to draw to itself whatever it conceives."[7] Collier's words were true sixty years ago, and they remain true today. We can accomplish great things if we determine our unique abilities and put them to work.

Not long ago I had a remarkable visit with a friend who coaches people in how to achieve optimum career success. He asked me what things I was best at doing. Without hesitation, I told him I was best at raising money for the college, creating innovative workforce initiatives, and marketing the college to the community.

His next question was, "How much of your time do you spend doing those things?" His question hit me like a brick. The truth is that I was spending an inordinate amount of time in administrative meetings, sometimes twelve or fifteen a day. My schedule was driving my staff and me almost beyond our capacity. As a result, I had become less effective in my work, and I was overworking my great team. The fiddler was playing faster and faster, and we just kept dancing faster. My friend's two simple questions served as a mental tipping point for me. Within two weeks my staff and I took a retreat with a facilitator to help us learn to focus on our unique abilities and prioritize our schedules and our work. We have made solid progress, and I am sure our productivity and the quality of our work have improved.

Most people know what they do well, but sometimes they need affirmation. You can ask your family and friends what they think you do best. Otherwise, try to remember why and how people compliment you. Repeated compliments by many different people are good indicators of your strengths. You might also reflect on the things you do that bring you the most satisfaction. Our unique abilities most often follow what we are happiest at doing. Discover your passion, and you will likely find your unique ability.

> Our unique abilities most often follow what we are happiest at doing. Discover your passion, and you will likely find your unique ability.

Keep in mind that you can also train yourself to become good at new things if you value the new things and expect that you can become good at doing them. I know plenty of people who became good cabinet makers or piano players after they retired. Of course, they valued the prospect of learning their new skills, and they had the confidence that they could be successful. The chances are good, however, that they probably had latent talent in woodworking and music since childhood. I could not write books until I trained myself in writing, but I always loved words and reading.

DISCOVER YOUR INTERESTS AND VALUES

I recommend that you consider taking a career aptitude test to gain insight into or affirm your unique ability. You can find good career assessments at your local library or at high schools and colleges. These assessments are designed to help you discover your interests, values, and abilities. We become good at the things we are interested in, the things we value, and the things for which we have a natural proclivity. As you compare probable careers to your interests, values, and abilities, the identification of a career focus will become increasingly evident.

When I ask people what they want to be doing in their careers in ten years, the question forces them to think about long-term planning, or if they already have a career vision for ten years out, it helps to reinforce their vision. The more you think about and talk about your career goal, the more likely it will happen. Another good question to ask yourself when considering a career path is, "Who do I wish to become?" This question forces you to review your purpose and your values by which you govern your life. Perhaps the easiest exercise in this vein is to pretend that you have a magic wand. Now, picture yourself at the height of your career when you have great personal success and deep respect from others. If you could have any job in the world, what would it be? The point of these exercises is to help you internalize what interests you and what you value.

I developed the following career assessment process for another book, *The 12 Essential Laws for Getting a Job . . . and Becoming Indispensable.*[8] It is also designed to help you discover your career interests and values. Take a blank piece of paper and title it "Interests."

1. List the activities and hobbies that make you the happiest. Now circle the three things that most interest you. As you begin to focus on your dream career, keep these interests in mind.

2. List six personal accomplishments of which you are most proud. These accomplishments can be ones that you achieved alone or with a team. Now review these accomplishments, and identify the particular part of each accomplishment that you most enjoyed. You should be able to discover a common theme or pattern among all the accomplishments. For example, did you most like working with others, or did you prefer to work alone? Were you most pleased at helping the organization achieve a goal or helping yourself achieve a goal? Your answers should provide insight into the things that interest you and whether you like working with others or alone.

Title a second sheet of paper "Values."

1. List the names of career professionals that you most admire.

2. Briefly describe the characteristics that you most admire about the people you listed.

3. Review your answers, and circle the top three people and the top three personal characteristics that you most admire. Keep these values in mind as you begin to shorten your dream career list.

Knowing what motivates you can also be helpful as you select your long-term career vision. You should be sure that your career field will provide plenty of opportunities for you to be motivated and fulfilled.

There are five primary motivators for today's American workers:

1. A sense of purpose
2. Recognition
3. A sense of belonging
4. Opportunity for personal growth
5. Fair compensation

As you consider a career field, think about what will provide you a sense of purpose, opportunities for recognition, a sense of belonging to a team, the opportunity for continued growth, and fair compensation. If one of these motivators is missing, you will be unhappy.

Two of my favorite motivational theories may be useful as you think about your career vision. The first theory, sometimes referred to as "expectancy theory," employs a formula that I have simplified to $M = EV$. It purports that a person is motivated (M) to action by his expectation (E) that he can be successful at a task or goal and by how much he values (V) the task or goal being considered.[9]

For example, I expect that I could sell television advertising well, but I would much rather work in higher education. On the other hand, I would really like to serve in the U.S. Senate, but I don't expect that I will ever be in the position to seriously run for that office. I am, therefore, not motivated to pursue either position. However, I really enjoy helping people obtain good jobs and excel at the workplace, and I had the expectation that I could write this book, so I proposed it to my publisher.

The second motivational theory that should be useful is the Poker Chip Theory of Self-Esteem.[10] It suggests that people will take risks to achieve bigger things only when they believe there is a high probability of success. If you have ever played poker, you know the feeling you get when you are winning and have stacks of poker chips in front of you. In this condition you will stay in a hand of poker, even if your first few cards show no promise. You are not afraid to take risks because you believe that you are on a roll or that you are really lucky. On the other hand, if you have been losing hand after hand and have only a few chips left, you are much less likely to take risks. You will wait until you have an unbeatable hand before risking your last chips.

People protect their self-esteem just as they protect their last chips in a poker game; they quit taking risks and just hope to maintain their current position. The odds of being dealt good cards or bad cards are the same for the winners and the losers. The only difference is their belief in themselves—their expectation of winning. You can compare your life's experiences to poker chips, where successes give you more chips and failures take away chips. Be sure to choose a career that will give you plenty of opportunities to collect many successes. And remember, the more you believe in yourself, the more you will grow and be successful in your career.

As I mentioned earlier, if you are not sure what careers are available, check out the North American Industry Classification System that lists all known jobs and career fields in North America. The Web site is www.census.gov/naics. Of course, you could always visit with a career counselor for assistance regarding possible careers.

Write down all your career ideas. Discuss them with people you admire, and choose the one you have the most passion about. Write down this long-term vision, and place it in a visible and prominent location. Read it often, and think about it every day. Visualize yourself doing what you ultimately intend, and expect that you will do well in your career.

DEVELOP YOUR CAREER PLAN

Once you home in on a career and determine the ultimate position you want to hold, you have to develop a plan. If you decided to drive from Cleveland to Martha's Vineyard for a vacation, wouldn't you consult a map? Building a successful career is infinitely more important to you and your family than one vacation, so give it very serious thought and develop your personal road map.

Most career fields already have some notable giants whom you could study. Lee Iacocca of the Chrysler Corporation became a giant in the automotive industry. Jack Welch of the General Electric Company was a legend in his field. Mary Kay Ash, of Mary Kay Cosmetics, set the standard for building an empire around her persona. Try to identify people in your chosen career field that you can study and emulate. You can be sure that Iacocca, Welch, and Ash also studied other people for insight in developing their career plans.

Most professions have fairly traditional pathways to success. To be a college president, you generally need to: have a doctorate, have taught successfully in your field, have been published, and be well-known and respected, and you must be a good fund-raiser and friend-raiser. Knowing this, I set a course toward earning my master's degree and doctorate as soon as I decided to be a community college president. I also began teaching myself how to be a better writer, and I read everything I could find about selling.

Network for Career Success

Networking with people in your chosen field is most helpful. Make a list of people you know who are in your chosen career field, and request an appointment with them. Most people will be happy to spend twenty or thirty minutes describing their career progress and giving you career advice. I probably talk to twenty-five or thirty people a year about my profession and how they can have successful careers. Networking should become a habit.

My twenty-four-year-old son thought he'd like to explore the real estate development business. We compiled a list of successful developers in both commercial and residential development, and he networked for six weeks. One developer told him to earn a real estate broker's license and then to call him for the next session after he had the license. He finished the course in record time, but in the meantime he took a new job on a trading floor of a large bank. He loves this new job, and his career plans have changed. He is now networking with people in higher positions in the banking industry.

Networking has multiple benefits. It helps you establish rapport with people in your chosen career field. It helps you assimilate a career path or plan to follow, and it helps you begin to think of yourself as someone who is already engaged in his or her career field. Companies don't hire people; people hire

> Companies don't hire people; people hire people.

people. You flatter most people when you talk with them about their careers, and they will have a tendency to mentor you if you stay close to them. Don't forget the thank-you notes!

Draw Your Own Blueprints for Success

After you have done your research and have focused on a specific long-term career goal, it is time to write out your plan. Identify the positions you will likely have to gain in order to achieve your long-term goal. You will also have to develop a time schedule for achieving each position. I've told you about my plan: At the age of twenty-two, I determined that with hard work I could become a community college president at age forty-four. I followed the plan, adjusted it as necessary, and became a president at age thirty-nine. Planning really does work!

Here is an easy outline for most career paths:

1. Set the career goal.
2. Network and research career paths.
3. Set job objectives with timelines.
4. Follow the plan.

Once you have established your long-term career goal and have researched the most probable path for obtaining it, you should write out specific interim objectives. These objectives must be measurable, for example: "My first objective is to complete a college degree in graphic arts. My second objective is to be employed in the graphic arts profession at entry level by January 10, 2007. My third objective is to become a graphic arts supervisor by January 10, 2008. My fourth objective is to open my own graphic arts business." You can adjust the game plan as you learn more about your professional field and about your abilities.

Be very specific about your career goals. When I first began hunting quail, I would sometimes shoot at the whole covey and come up with no birds. It was astonishing to me that I didn't hit anything. My father explained that "flock shooting" will seldom bag a bird. He taught me to focus on one bird at a time. As in bird hunting, people who are moving toward their career goals should focus on one job at a time.

My first occupational objective was to be employed as a speech teacher in a high school. My second objective was to become a teacher in higher education. These objectives were followed by becoming a department head, division director, dean, vice president for instruction, and finally president. Of course, each position required additional degrees or specified training. You have to have a master's degree before becoming a faculty member in higher education, and a doctorate is preferred before you can expect to become a vice president. Nearly every career field will have specific requirements and skills necessary for increasingly more responsible positions.

Some people also attach a monetary component to their progressive career objectives. There is certainly nothing wrong with setting monetary goals, but the most successful professionals I know will tell you that they viewed the size of their salary as a by-product for doing a great job. Their first objectives were getting the next-level job and excelling at it. It follows that if your work is exemplary, you will continue to be promoted and will receive increased compensation.

VISUALIZE SUCCESS, CONQUER DOUBT

The Highest Rungs Are Reached by Engaging in Continuous Self-Improvement

One natural part of the human experience is to strive for self-improvement. As you achieve one career objective, you should celebrate, but immediately begin preparing for the next objective. This is true for anyone who understands that life provides ever-expanding growth opportunities.

Politicians are acutely aware of this personal development cycle. A typical politician will run for the school board. After a term or two, he will seek election to the city council or the county commission. After a term or two, he will run for the legislature, and so forth. All successful professionals view their careers in the same manner.

Along the way, you will inevitably hit a barrier or experience a setback as you attempt to work your career plan. Most of us have occasional blasts of insecurity or doubt about achieving the next job objective. When I became the chief academic officer of a college, I was thrilled for about the first hour, then reality hit me. I began to have a few humbling thoughts about my ability to handle such a weighty job. The more I dwelled on my new responsibilities, the more insecure I became. This anxiety was healthy in that it forced me to think better and gather more information before making decisions. On the other hand, I am sure my anxiety was evident until I became more secure in the job. Subordinates tend to model the behavior of their supervisors, and they need to feel secure by knowing that their supervisors are secure.

You really are vulnerable whenever you take on new responsibilities, but don't let them intimidate you. You wouldn't have been placed in the job unless your superiors thought you were ready for it. Besides, those who promoted or hired you want you to succeed. Their reputation is also connected to your performance, and they will help you succeed. You can also reduce your insecurities and help guarantee success by quickly building trusting relationships. The more your subordinates know you trust and care for them, the more they will trust and care for you. The same is true for your superiors, peers, and customers. This principle of reciprocity is so important that I have dedicated a whole chapter to it.

> You really are vulnerable whenever you take on new responsibilities, but don't let them intimidate you. You wouldn't have been placed in the job unless your superiors thought you were ready for it.

There is no better security than that which comes from being knowledgeable and practiced in your field. However, another method for removing self-doubt and becoming secure in your progression up the career ladder is to learn to visualize yourself as being successful in your long-term career goal. The ability to clearly create a mental picture of how you want to be or what you want to become is a secret to success. Claude Bristol wrote a fascinating book titled *The Magic of Believing*. Bristol presented a compelling argument that our subconscious minds help us solve problems and achieve goals, but the process works ever so much better if our conscious minds can first imagine a mental picture of what we desire.[11]

I once produced a fishing program for the public broadcasting station I was privileged to manage. In the mid-1970s, professional bass fishing was getting started in a big way in the southern United States, and Tom Mann was an early professional tournament great. Tom had done so well and had become so popular that he seized the day by creating his own fishing lure company. His Jelly Worms were a big hit, and he was soon one of the largest fishing lure manufacturers in the world. Through a mutual friend I was able to film a show about Tom and his brother at Lake Eufaula on the Georgia-Alabama line. I will never forget Tom's answer to my question about how he had become the greatest fisherman of his time. "I expect to catch a big bass on every cast!" was his reply. "I am never surprised by a strike, and I therefore have fewer misses."

I also asked him how he had become so successful in the lure manufacturing business. His reply was essentially the same: "I believed I could produce better products than my competitors." The lesson to be learned is that our expectations and our beliefs are critical components to future success. Keeping a positive attitude about our capabilities is a prescription for success.

Over the years I have learned to believe I will find a parking place whenever I need one. Now I expect to find a convenient parking place wherever I go. I visualize finding a good spot even if the parking lot or parking garage is usually full. Since I expect to find a good spot to park, I almost always do. I feel the same way about my career. Certainly I realize that there will be challenges at work, but deep down I always know things will work out. What you visualize and believe is what you will generally get. If you fret over finding a place to park, you usually won't find one. If you doubt that you can handle work challenges, you probably won't handle them well.

BE TOO BUSY WINNING TO LOSE

One of life's paradoxes is the principle of perpetual growth or continuous expansion. We are meant to have life and have it in abundance, but only if we recognize that we must continue to seek improvement and expand our influence and resources. Once we stop growing or expanding, we begin to focus on holding on to what we have achieved. Eventually doubt creeps into the psyche, and we lose confidence because we become afraid of losing something as opposed to getting excited about gaining something. By its nature, the former position is negative, while the growth position is positive. The message is to continue expanding our minds, influence, and resources throughout life. We must resist the temptation to rest on past laurels.

James is one of the most remarkable human beings I have ever met. You wouldn't know him, but you are likely to if he continues his growth and expansion. In 1994, when he was in his late thirties, James was living at the men's homeless shelter in Charlotte, North Carolina. He had no job, no money, and no future, but he realized that his ticket to self-sufficiency rested with his ability to improve his education. He had deficiencies in math and English and had not finished high school. He boarded our college's van one day and asked to sign up for the General Equivalency Diploma (GED) program.

We bused James and fellow shelter residents to the college on a daily basis. James never ceased to work hard toward his goal of getting a high school equivalent diploma. After a few months, he passed the GED test and enrolled in the college transfer program. James was learning the principle of continued expansion. He completed his two-year associate in arts degree and enrolled at the University of North Carolina at Charlotte.

In two more years, James finished his teaching degree at the university, and we hired him to teach basic skills in our GED program. The student had become the teacher. James continued his education by finishing his master's degree last year, and I recently wrote a glowing letter of recommendation for him to enter the university's doctoral program. Along the way James got married, bought a house, and became a monthly columnist for the *Charlotte Observer*! James understands the value of perpetual growth and the importance of visualizing his goals. He also never let self-doubt or insecurity overcome his progress. As another student once told me, he was "too busy winning to lose!"

That's the message for you—be too busy winning to lose. Focus on the progressive expansion of your career to achieve your ultimate career vision. There is great power in vision, but you also have to execute your career plan and continue visualizing and believing you will achieve each progressive step. To achieve is to believe in yourself and to stay focused on the goal. And that's what the next chapter is about, helping you learn how to control your thoughts for unbelievable career success!

| LADDER-BUILDING TIPS |

1. Get a solid sense of who you are, and know what you want to become.
2. Understand and believe in the power of vision.
3. Discover your unique abilities.
4. Set a grand vision for your career.
5. Develop a career plan for achieving your vision.
6. Visualize your successes and continue growing.

| LADDER-BUILDING ACTIONS |

1. My long-term grand career vision is to become

_____

_____

2. I will begin my path toward achieving this vision by
   (*a*) achieving the necessary credentials of _____ and
   (*b*) getting an ascending number of jobs beginning with

   _____,
   (*c*) followed by these positions: _____,
   _____, and _____.
3. I will be employed in my first career job on or before _____.
4. I will achieve my pinnacle job of _____ on or before

   _____.
5. I recognize that I am master of my own career and that a commitment to this career plan is essential for success.
6. I further understand the importance of being focused on the future, visualizing my goals, and continuing to grow in my career.

Signed _____

Date _____

| 3 |

THE POWER OF THOUGHT

We Become What We Think

*It is impossible to think of one thing
and produce another.*
—Emmet Fox

LET'S THINK ABOUT IT

Eagle Scouts understand their responsibility to set a high moral example with their lives. Through their training, they come to think of themselves as achievers and persons dedicated to serving others. In consequence, they serve others and become lifelong achievers. In fact, the world also thinks that Eagle Scouts must provide a good example for living. If an Eagle Scout commits some criminal infraction, the newspaper will always enhance the fact that he was an Eagle Scout because of the inconsistency in expected behavior. Most Eagle Scouts, and the world, have come to follow the behaviors that they think about and know are expected of them.

We are the sum total of what we think about. Nothing can be accomplished without a preceding thought. We cannot expect to have productive and successful careers or lives without understanding the power of thought and how to use this most wonderful resource for good. The Bible states, "For as he thinks within himself, so he is."[1] Successful people have learned how to think well! The purpose of this chapter is to help you understand the power of thought and how to use this blessing to your advantage.

Before we attempt to learn about anything, we must study it in its natural context and analyze our relationship to it. The same is true with the study of thought. What is it? Who can have it? How is it done? What can it achieve? Where does it come from? Why do we have it? When can it be done? We must approach this brief study of a phenomenally complex topic recognizing our limited understanding of it. Please be assured that there is more that we don't understand about thinking and how it works than what we do understand. Nevertheless, if we can begin to recognize the power of thought and use it to our advantage, our career goals and life in general will benefit.

Researchers have long wondered how the brain actually works. Bear in mind that it is exceedingly difficult for a bodily organ to study itself. Yet we do know more about the brain than ever before. For example, contrary to common belief, we do not lose brain cells as we grow older as long as they continue to be stimulated through use. Recent research indicates that there is no difference between a twenty-five-year-old brain and a seventy-five-year-old brain if both brains are healthy.[2]

We also know that the brain is like any other part of the body in that it must be used to work well. Just as we must do for a muscle, we either use it or lose it! Evidence indicates that the more the brain is stimulated, the better it works. To stay sharp, you must continue thinking and learning. The following brain stimulation factors appear to help people stay bright and keep good memories:

1. Having an above-average education
2. Having no chronic disease
3. Being engaged in reading, travel, and new experiences
4. Being willing to change
5. Being gratified with accomplishments
6. Being married to a smart spouse[3]

Brain cells, which are often called *neurons*, analyze, coordinate, and transmit information. Learning and memory—indeed the ability to think—occur through billions of connections called *synapses*. Interestingly, these memory synapses, or pathways, can disappear if they are not used. The opposite is also true. The more we think, the better we get at thinking! Successful people are good thinkers.

You might remember from your studies that small electrochemical actions occur as neurotransmitters (molecules) jump across a small gap between the axons (transmitters) and the dendrites (receivers) in the brain. This activity takes place when the brain sends signals to some part of the body, when we sense something from our environment, or when we think. To be sure, our genes determine much about our brains, but our environment, especially during the first five years, provides the instructions and final development of our brains.[4] People can continue to learn and even become smarter as they age if they keep their brains engaged and stimulated.

We exist in a physical environment of space and time, where reality is primarily what we can perceive with our senses. If we can see it, touch it, smell it, taste it, or feel it, it is real to us. We also live in a spiritual dimension that can be complementary to the more prevalent physical dimension we know so well. Theologians make a compelling case that we live in both dimensions until our physical existence is over, and then we live completely in the spiritual dimension. Some scientists suggest that we live completely in a physical dimension. In either case, we still have the gift of independent thought and the ability to make good choices.

There do seem to be universal laws that influence and affect all human beings. On the physical side, we have gravity, heat, cold, and other laws that will become excellent learning experiences if you violate them. If you use them to your advantage, they can be your best friends. The same is true with nonphysical or spiritual laws. If you think badly of others, your demeanor will reflect your thoughts, and others will perceive it and eventually think badly of you. If you have faith in God, you will always have a loving Companion. Thinking is reciprocal.

William Arthur Ward stated, "Nothing limits achievement like small thinking; nothing expands possibilities like unleashed thinking." We create our own circumstances by how we think and what we think about. We can sow good thoughts and reap good things, or we can sow bad thoughts and reap bad things.

Our ultimate freedom as human beings is the freedom of thought. Those who learn to control their thoughts are those who are most successful in their careers and in life. *Good thinking is a learned skill. It doesn't happen automatically.* However, you can learn to think well by understanding the relationships among your thoughts, feelings, and desires. Once you learn to separate rational thoughts from ego-centered thoughts, you are well on your way to becoming a good thinker.

THOUGHTS DRIVE BEHAVIOR

Consider this point. Our thoughts determine our feelings (which affect our perceptions) and our beliefs (which drive our behavior). Over time, our behavior becomes habitual, and it defines our character. Ultimately our thoughts and beliefs determine who we become and drive us to our destiny. If you can learn to objectively control your thoughts, you can become whatever you desire.

Drs. Linda Elder and Richard Paul have written extensively on the subjects of creative and analytical thinking. One publication presents humans as having three distinctive functions: thinking, feeling, and wanting. Their research suggests that our thinking is influenced greatly by our feelings and our desires. This is ego-centered and emotionally driven thinking. Rational thinking can occur when we intentionally separate our feelings and desires from the situation being thought about. Rational thinking involves placing yourself in an objective rather than subjective point of view, analyzing and clarifying until you can make a comfortable and logical choice or take appropriate action.[5]

My father was fond of saying, "If you don't like the facts, change your attitude about them." That was a good way of suggesting that we can live happier lives if we learn to alter our perceptions about our circumstances. He was advising us to think rationally, putting aside our feelings and our desires. Some years ago I was sharing an aggravating circumstance with two community college colleagues. A university president told me he could not partner with our community college because it would be bad for the university's image. I perceived his statement as being elitist and generally uncooperative. I was hoping to get some sympathy from my community college colleagues, but to my surprise, one of them said he agreed with the university president and said that I should try to see it from his point of view. That was a bitter pill to swallow, but once I separated my feelings, including the desire to partner, from my thinking, I was able to see his point of view. I remembered that the university president was lobbying the state's policy makers to allow his school to move from a regional university to a research university. I could agree that a high-profile association with an undergraduate two-year teaching college would be bad timing for a university that was trying to emerge as a research institution.

When I was a very young father, I experienced a revelation about how I thought. Our son, Brett, was in his terrible twos, nothing seemed to satisfy him, and it was my turn to watch him all afternoon. He was constantly asking for this and that, and I wanted to finish reading a magazine story. In a frenzy I shouted, "Have some patience!" In a flash of insight, I listened to my words and was convicted. I was the one with no patience, and he was acting like a normal child. Once I separated my feelings and desires from the situation and focused on my son instead of myself, I could deal with it on a rational basis. We both had a better time after that. As we progress through our career goals, we must learn to think rationally and try to see things from everyone's point of view.

I advise my senior officers to approach every meeting by understanding its purpose, what they hope to get out of it, and how they expect to achieve their goal for the meeting. In effect, I ask them to think about the most probable positions each attendee will take and to consider a way for each person to achieve his goals. The art of negotiation is not about who wins or loses; it is about creating a winning situation for everyone. This can be done only through rational thinking.

I love to sell things: ideas, scholarship endowments, books, and the like. I never think that I am making a sale, though. I always think about how I am giving people the opportunity to help themselves or, in the case of the scholarship endowment, the opportunity to become significant and feel good about themselves. But even then, I study the prospects beforehand to determine what their feelings and desires are likely to be, and I match my appeal to what they will receive well based on what they value.

BELIEFS REINFORCE THEMSELVES

We have a tendency to perceive things in a way that reinforces our existing beliefs. Witnesses to a crime often describe the criminal in vastly different ways. People can listen to the same speaker and come away with opposite impressions because we filter thoughts and ideas according to preconceived notions and beliefs.

My wife and I were once guests at a dinner with the world-renowned Lech Walesa. He was a charming person, and we all felt special to have such an intimate time with this famous person. When dinner was over, he spoke to the group of about twenty-five people. After the usual courtesies, he told us that America was the greatest economic power in the world and should therefore be responsible for the world and its economy. He further told us that we should change our free enterprise system and convert to a socialistic system in order to provide economic justice to the world. He was speaking through an interpreter and paused at that point for effect. To our astonishment, the entire crowd, except for my wife and me, applauded vigorously. (I never cease to wonder why people can look at the United States, the greatest economic power in the world, and think we should become more socialistic. They can't name one place where socialism has been successful, but somehow they think it's superior to capitalism.) I guess they heard something we didn't hear, or we heard something they didn't hear. Then again, it could have been that people were so enamored with him that they didn't listen at all. In any event, the story illustrates how things can be perceived differently by different people. *You will help your career a great deal if you can learn to see and listen with discernment regardless of your environment.*

As a college president, I have to please a number of constituencies, including politicians. Most politicians want to do a good job for their constituents, but they are often biased by their hard-core political beliefs. Before I address any policy makers, I think about their point of view and alter my approach to them accordingly. If I am seeking more money for the college from Republicans, I stress the value of the college from an economic development perspective. If I am addressing Democrats, I stress the value of the college to its students and the families who are so positively affected. To the Republicans, a return on investment is important. To the Democrats, the humanitarian aspects of the college are important. I am not compromising any personal beliefs, because both points of view are worthy and significant for students and our community. When I speak to Republicans and Democrats jointly, I speak about both the economic and the human development value of the college, and both groups have their political feelings and desires reinforced.

LEARNING TO LEARN

I have been studying about learning and learners for thirty-five years. The teaching and learning process is the essence of the education profession. If students don't learn, education has not occurred. Today, we must be lifelong learners. The rapid changes in technology and the globalization of the economy demand that we continue learning to stay up to date in our occupational fields. We must develop an internal motivation to be lifelong learners. If we hope to be leaders in our fields, we also have to be the best learners. Besides, the more we learn, the smarter we become. Ron Harper, a great friend of mine and an eminently successful businessman, recently wrote his memoirs, and he titled his book *The Harder I Work, the Luckier I Get*. It is a wonderful title, but it would have been more accurate if he had named it *The Harder I Think, the Luckier I Get* or *The More I Learn, the Luckier I Get*. In any event, the person who develops a healthy appetite for learning is lucky indeed!

James Zull, in his book *The Art of Changing the Brain,* says that learning, a process of thought, is a physical activity. He states that biological activity changes the brain when learning occurs. New brain connections, called *synapses,* occur when something is learned and can be remembered.[6] Teachers can influence students' ability to learn by creating favorable conditions for learning. We know that students learn best by participating in the learning process. Listening to a lecture is the least-effective condition for learning, yet, for teachers, it has been the preferred delivery method for hundreds of years. Listening and seeing a demonstration is a better method for learning something, but actually doing the activity is best of all. The best way to learn to change a tire is to participate in changing one; the best way to learn the alphabet is to practice it out loud, write the letters, sing the alphabet song, and engage in any number of additional activities. The truth is that learners know how to learn on their own, and they can teach themselves to learn even better.

Learning is simply experiencing something, reflecting on it, associating it with similar things previously learned, and putting what you have learned into practice. We categorize learning into three domains: cognitive, psychomotor, or affective. Some things we learn are simply knowledge (cognitive), like understanding how to multiply numbers. Other things we learn are physically based (psychomotor) skills primarily involving the use of our bodies, like casting a fishing line. We also learn to experience emotion or feelings (we're affected) under certain conditions, like jealousy. Of course, all three domains are usually influencing one another as we perform some function. As you approach a subject, it is useful to first learn the knowledge needed to think a certain way or to perform some action; next, practice the desired thinking or action; and then assess how you feel about it. If you gain pleasure for the experience, you will be motivated to learn even more.

While living in Colorado, I determined I would learn to fly-fish. The streams were beautiful, and I loved to bait cast for bass, but the preferred fishing in Colorado was to fly-fish for trout. I first talked to people who already knew how to fly-fish. With their encouragement, I read a book on fly-casting and another on knot tying needed for fly-fishing. I mentally compared fly-fishing to bait casting and determined there was very little in common with the two fishing techniques. In my backyard my neighbor explained about the necessary equipment I would need and demonstrated how to cast. Best of all, he took me fishing on the Arkansas River. As I waded in the shallows of that beautiful river and caught my first rainbow trout, I was euphoric. I have been an avid trout fisherman since that day some twenty years ago.

My instincts told me I should learn to fly-fish because there was little bass fishing in Colorado and because I liked being out of doors. After gaining the knowledge to do the basics, I participated in the activity. That participation produced pleasurable emotions, and I am still learning more and more about the sport. I still read about it, talk about it, and do it whenever possible. More important, I am still motivated to learn even more about this fascinating sport.

Most of us have preferred learning methods. Astute teachers have known for years that there are three preferred learning styles. There are those who learn best by listening, those who learn best by seeing, and those who learn best by doing. A combination of all three styles is generally most effective. But if you learn well by listening, start listening to books and self-help CDs. If you learn best by sight, buy and watch videos. If you learn best through action, as most of us do, by all means do it physically. The most effective learning occurs when your preferred style is complemented by a secondary style.

If you have chosen a career goal about which you are passionate, you will have the internal motivation to be a continuous learner about your field. The best people in any field are those who have the most knowledge and experience about it. Be sure your chosen occupational field is something you really enjoy.

THINKING FOR GOOD OR BAD

For every action there is a reaction. For every choice there is a consequence. Be careful about your thinking, because it yields reactions and consequences. Our thoughts manifest themselves in action, whether we want them to or not. The world without is a reflection of the world within. Experiences and conditions are effects, and thoughts are the causes.[7]

If you plant tomatoes in your garden, should you expect to harvest grapes? If you plant weeds, should you expect to reap turnips? Our thoughts return in kind. If we think and wish for good things, good things we will get. If we sow negative and self-ish thoughts, the same will be returned to us.

The opportunities for you to achieve the life and career you want are limitless. Your subconscious mind will follow orders from your thoughts, whether they are good or bad. Hitler was a good thinker, but he misused his God-given gift in terrible ways. Winston Churchill was a good thinker, and he used his gift for good. At some point, both individuals chose how they would use their mental energies. You can consciously choose to do your thinking for good or for bad.

The more a potential thief thinks about the rewards of steal-ing, the more likely he will commit the theft. Eventually he will steal something. If the rewards, in his mind, are worth the risk, he will continue stealing. After a while, stealing becomes a habit and then an addiction. The thief enjoys the high he gets from stealing. This emotional high is chemically created by the brain when he steals. His thoughts have manifested themselves into habitual action, which produces the emotional high, which reinforces the behavior to the point that it becomes addictive.

How many famous people are addicted to shoplifting? They have plenty of money, and they usually don't even want or need the items they steal. They have become addicted, just like compulsive gamblers. But what can the addicted thief or gambler do to help himself? First, he should get professional counseling, but no compulsive behavior is changed unless the person wants to change and begins to think in different ways. If he can substitute stealing for something good that produces a similar emotional high, he has a solid chance of completely changing from bad to good habits.

I believe we cannot effect permanent change unless we experience a significant emotional event or unless we can tie our new desired behavior to some preexisting core value. We all know people who became devoutly religious as a result of some significant emotional event. Others are able to change bad habits by acknowledging that the habits are in conflict with a core moral value that represents who they wish to become. If one truly loves God, yet cheats on his wife, he will suffer from this conflict of values versus behavior. At some point, he will surrender to his moral values or to his temptations. This is the great internal struggle of life, and each of us must deal with it.

If you can become mentally and emotionally addicted to things that are bad for you and those around you, can you become addicted to things that are good for you and others? The answer is a resounding yes! Volunteers who serve in their churches or at soup kitchens or in hospitals get emotional reinforcement from helping others. One man here in North Carolina has held a Thanksgiving Day feast for the homeless for more than twenty years, and he is now serving hundreds of needy people each year. I would say he is addicted to doing that good thing for his fellow man. Feeding the needy has become part of his character. I would also guess that at some point he chose to do something for those less fortunate because this behavior reinforced his desire to serve God. You see, it is all up to you. You alone are responsible for yourself and your behavior. Think about it.

As discussed earlier, our beliefs also affect how we think. If we believe a thing, it is difficult to change that belief, because beliefs become part of our value system, and our value system represents our core being. We are generally egocentric beings, and we have a natural tendency to ignore facts and evidence that contradict our favored beliefs and values. We also have a tendency to cite and remember evidence that supports our beliefs.[8] When we cannot separate our beliefs from our thoughts, it is difficult to achieve objectivity and rational thinking.

A wise approach is to look at something from all points of view to see it clearly. That's why we share our thoughts and ideas with others before making a decision. Our oldest son was recently being recruited to open and manage a new upscale restaurant, which was very tempting to him. He agonized over this offer, since he already had a good job and was secure in it. He was wise enough to discuss his dilemma before making a choice. After presenting the pros and cons as he saw them, he asked for input from the rest of the family. We gave him our best thinking, and I am sure he was better prepared to make a choice because our thoughts added to his body of knowledge about that choice. In the end it was his decision, but his rational mind knew he needed help in viewing the situation from all vantage points. He took the new job.

We develop beliefs from family tradition and from listening to respected opinion leaders such as a preacher, teacher, or elected official, or we conclude something strongly based on our own analysis and experience. These fundamental beliefs can be your best friends or your worst enemies. If you honestly believe you can achieve something, you will be able to achieve it. If, deep down, you believe you aren't capable of achieving it, you will fail. The more you can eliminate these self-defeating beliefs, the more successful you will become.

> If you honestly believe you can achieve something, you will be able to achieve it. If, deep down, you believe you aren't capable of achieving it, you will fail. The more you can eliminate these self-defeating beliefs, the more successful you will become.

THINK TO THINK BETTER

You may be thinking, *But I have never been good at school,* or, *I'm not bright enough to be a good thinker.* My mentor and good friend Zig Ziglar calls this "stinkin' thinkin'." I can't think of a better name for negative thinking. Negative thinking will produce negative results. Thoughts, whether negative or positive, produce identical actions or attitudes. If you believe you do not have the capacity to become a good thinker, you will not become a good thinker. The opposite is true, of course, so you should make the choice easily. The key is to believe in yourself enough to take the risk of trying. Remember our discussion on how the brain gets better at thinking by thinking? Try it; you'll like it!

Leadership expert John Maxwell states, "It doesn't matter whether you were born rich or poor. It doesn't matter if you have a third grade education or possess a Ph.D. It doesn't matter if you suffer from multiple disabilities or you're the picture of health. No matter what your circumstances, you can learn to be a good thinker. All you must do is be willing to engage in the process every day."[9] This is great advice. Anyone whose brain is not diseased or adversely affected in some debilitating way can learn to think well. I have seen young students and old students take control of their lives once they learn that they can think for themselves. You have the equipment; all you have to do is to create the personal motivation to work at it.

There are many types of thinking, including creative thinking, contemplative thinking, critical thinking, anticipatory thinking, and reminiscent thinking. It has been my experience that my best thinking happens when I am without distractions. In fact, my best thinking comes when I am taking a shower or driving alone. At work, my best thinking occurs when I walk around the room and verbalize my thoughts. You should place yourself in whatever circumstance makes you the most comfortable while trying to think. And by the way, don't distract yourself with unwanted or irrelevant thoughts. Good thinking is focused thinking.

It's Smart to Create Uniqueness in Your Career

Don't you love being around creative thinkers? They have practiced thinking about innovative and creative ways of doing things or building things. They may be poets or actors or inventors. Whatever their vocation, they seem to be the people who come up with unique ideas first. They may have a genetic proclivity for being creative thinkers, but anyone can become good at being creative in his thinking. Read books about inventors and other creative people. Think about what you would do to improve something in your company or organization if you had a magic wand. Place yourself in group meetings where the purpose is to be creative. Each person's thoughts help the others think more creatively. As you practice solving problems with others or writing poetry alone, creative thinking gets easier as your brain grows accustomed to thinking in this manner.

Think It Through

Contemplative thinking is usually done in private. It is a meditative state when one ponders something or gives something thoughtful consideration. Do not confuse contemplative thinking with the New Age Meditation techniques that were popular to some, especially in the seventies.

Much of our thinking involves serious analytical attention, such as when we try to make a good decision. Again, get into a comfortable place without distractions, and your meditations will be fruitful. People who go through life being buffeted by every circumstance will continue leading reactive instead of proactive lives unless they can contemplate their situation and change their thinking. You can bet James, the GED-to-doctoral student I mentioned earlier, contemplated his circumstance and decided to change his thinking. When his thinking changed, he changed, and he is now leading a happy, productive life instead of an unhappy, unproductive one. Remember that learning involves change and change involves learning.

> People who go through life being buffeted by every circumstance will continue leading reactive instead of proactive lives unless they can contemplate their situation and change their thinking.

Critical Thinking

Critical thinking is getting a great deal of interest from educators these days because it provides a first-rate model for learning to learn well. Critical thinking involves the ability to respond to material or circumstances in a rational, nonjudgmental manner. This type of thinking enables the thinker to distinguish between facts and opinions or emotions. It allows the thinker to be objective in reasoning and to make choices based on logic and fact. In effect, critical thinkers learn to take charge of their own thinking and arrive at their own conclusions.

Allen Tate is a great friend and a mentor whom I admire for his thinking and his huge success in real estate. The Tate Realty Company is one of the largest private real estate firms in the country, conducting more than $4 billion in business each year. I once asked Allen what made his company so successful. Without hesitation, he told me it was his ability to anticipate the future in his vocation. He surmised early in his career that the only way to beat his competition was to outthink them. He began by learning to anticipate what market influences would likely occur in the immediate and longer-term future. He was good at it and got better. While owners of most real estate companies were pushing their people to get listings and sell property, Allen was recruiting and retaining the best realtors in the marketplace. While others were just selling homes, Allen was providing quality living and convenience by adding relocation services, mortgage assistance, and home maintenance services as additional options for his customers. Learning to anticipate the future direction of your business or occupation can be a huge advantage to your future success.

Reminiscent thinking involves reflecting on past situations to help make good decisions today. That old quote by George Santayana is true: "Those who cannot remember the past are condemned to repeat it." You have millions of experiences and lessons learned to draw upon for help when you need to make a decision or think through something. Sometimes reminiscent thinking is done in groups, just for fun. Do you remember when candy bars cost only a nickel?

Practice makes perfect. Try learning to become more aware of your environment to help your thinking. For example, the next time you watch a movie, try to become more engaged rather than just passively enjoying the event. Ask yourself why the screenplay writer began with the first scene as he did. Was it because that scene set the tone for the entire movie, or was it used simply to get the audience's attention quickly? Ask yourself what appears to be motivating each character to behave as he or she does. How has the writer built suspense? How did the director contribute to the suspense? Was the angle of the camera shot important, and did the music crescendo at just the right time? The more you become engaged, the more you will discover about the film. You will soon be seeing subplots and intelligence behind shots and scenes and characters that you would have missed had you sat being passively entertained.

You can do the same thing every day as you communicate with others. Be focused, be a good listener, and be engaged. Think about the impression you want to make and how you want to influence others; then do those things you think will project the impression or influence them the most. Think about their words, and respond in ways that will benefit them. Think about their point of view, and be helpful in ways that will surprise them. Send them a note about something that impressed you about them or just a note of thanks for the time together.

As you practice being in tune with your surroundings and being more receptive to stimuli in social situations, it will get easier. As with most things, after you practice something for about a month, it becomes a habit. Before you know it, you will be receiving and analyzing more information in any given circumstance than ever before. This heightened awareness of your environment and others will give you more information to process and a better reference point from which to respond and make decisions. In effect, you will become a better thinker and make better responses and choices.

| LADDER-BUILDING TIPS |

1. Thoughts are things.
2. Thoughts manifest themselves for good or bad.
3. Thoughts create beliefs and emotions that can influence thought.
4. Good thinking is learned.

| LADDER-BUILDING ACTIONS |

1. From this day forward I will become more aware of how I perceive and think about things that can support or limit my career success. I will do this by

_____

_____

_____

2. I will consciously work to learn to think more rationally and logically by

_____

_____

_____

3. I recognize that most career limitations are self-imposed. I will consciously work to eliminate the fears, doubts, and beliefs that limit me. List the fears, doubts, and beliefs here:

_____

_____

_____

| 4 |

THE MIND-BODY CONNECTION

The happiness of your life depends
upon the quality of your thoughts.
—Marcus Antoninus

MIND-BODY CONNECTION

In the fall of 1967, I was a frightened but gung ho student teacher in Lawrence Central High School just east of Indianapolis. Like most of my college pals, I smoked. Everyone in the teacher's lounge also smoked, or so it seemed. My supervising teacher taught me a good many things about how to handle a classroom and how to prepare a lesson plan, but the best lesson I learned was on the last day of my student teaching semester. She called me into her office and told me I had the ability to become a good teacher, but only if I kept my health. "Smokers inevitably lose their health, and then all their hopes, dreams, and skills are useless," she said. "You must make a conscious effort to nurture your body just as you nurture your mind!" I took her advice and haven't smoked for more than thirty years.

Successful people understand the importance of staying in balance physically, mentally, spiritually, and emotionally. They recognize that they must have harmony in their lives in order to be effective and to remain healthy. For decades now the research is irrefutable that the mind in large part controls the body. If the mind is distressed or preoccupied with negative thoughts or fear, the body is affected, especially when the emotions are repressed. Our minds and bodies are integrated, and even our health is affected by our thinking.

Dr. Wayne Dyer stated this in his book *Staying on the Path*: "When you think positive, happy, loving thoughts, there's a different chemistry that goes into your body than when you think depressing, negative, anguished thoughts. The way you decide to think has a dramatic effect on your chemistry and on your physiology."[1]

Remember Viktor Frankl's testimony that there was a mind-body connection among the prisoners of his concentration camp? Those who lost courage and hope also lost their health.[2] American Institute of Stress researchers estimate that 75 to 90 percent of all visits to health-care providers result from stress-related disorders. Emotional stress most likely doesn't cause the illness but creates vulnerability in the body's immune system, which makes us more susceptible to disease.[3]

DEALING WITH JOB STRESS

We hear so much about the negative consequences of job stress these days that it has become a major health concern for most organizations. Some studies demonstrate a high correlation between job stress and heart disease.[4] Certainly some jobs are more stressful than others, and there are circumstances, such as an unfair supervisor or unrealistic deadlines, that cause emotional distress. But in the end, it is how we respond to the stressful situation that is important. It is not what happens *to* us, but what happens *in* us that is important.

A certain amount of stress is healthy and provides focus and a competitive edge. It energizes us and motivates us to solve problems and meet challenges. Without some stress, work would have little meaning and would be no fun. However, too much stress for too long a period will cause damage if we don't limit the source of the stress or make sure our response to it is rational. If we are consumed with ourselves and view the world as either for or against us, our response to stress will probably be unhealthy. Egocentric people tend to view every negative thing as personal when most things are actually situational. A rational thinker will analyze the situation, see it for what it is, and then decide whether it is something on which he should take action. *One of the most damaging things you can do to yourself in stressful situations is to begin imagining that the worst will happen.* Such imaginings are normal but are destructive and of no benefit; besides, the worst very seldom happens.

> If we are consumed with ourselves and view the world as either for or against us, our response to stress will probably be unhealthy. Egocentric people tend to view every negative thing as personal when most things are actually situational.

You may choose from numerous books and articles about how to handle job stress. Most of them will advise that you prioritize your work, take frequent breaks, and eliminate any meetings or work that you don't need to fulfill the responsibilities of your job. The most important advice, however, is to learn to view your job from afar. Once you see your job from the thirty-thousand-foot level, it will cease to be the most critical job in the world. Much of your job stress comes from the idea that you must control everything and strive to perform better month after month. Unhealthy job stress also comes from the fear that you will lose your job or your reputation. I have found it helpful to look at every stressful situation and put it in perspective by asking these questions:

1. Does this situation threaten my soul?
2. Does this situation threaten my life?
3. Does this situation threaten my family?
4. Does this situation threaten my job?
5. How important will I think this situation is next week, next month, next year?

You get the point. A little warning flag should go up every time you feel stressed. Dr. Herbert Benson of Harvard Medical School has been researching the effects of the mind on the body for decades. His book, *The Relaxation Response,* has helped millions of people learn the art of self-care. His research indicates that people who learn to recognize stressful situations and respond to them rationally stay healthier than those who don't learn to control stressful situations.[5]

When we find ourselves in unhealthy, stressful situations, we generally move into the "fight or flight" mode: the adrenaline surges, the heart rate increases, and we are poised to take action. Dr. Benson advocates a response of relaxation rather than preparing to fight or take flight. I have found him to be right. For example, when I am in a stressful or potentially stressful situation, I can feel my heart rate increase and my body begin to stiffen. That is a clear signal for me to take a deep breath and think of the word *relax* or the words *be still.* Like magic, my heart rate returns to normal, and I am relaxed. If I give in to my emotions in such a situation, I am doing harm to myself and probably aggravating the circumstance that produced the response rather than helping to minimize the situation.

Since our thinking about a problem produces negative emotions, we can change or minimize such emotional responses by changing how we think about stressful problems. Psychologists call this process *behavior modification.* Dr. Benson calls it a process for self-help. The name doesn't matter, but it is important for everyone to learn to control negative responses to stressful situations.

But how do you control your response to a supervisor who constantly tries to persecute you? Changing jobs would be one answer, but you would probably run into another poorly developed supervisor in the next job. My mother would advise that you cover that person with kindness. My father would advocate changing your attitude about him. I have found both reactions to be effective, especially if I pray for that person and for his ability to become a great supervisor and do well. It is hard for someone to mistreat you if you are kind to him, and it is even harder for him to hurt you if you have no malice toward him. It is especially difficult to stay angry at someone for whom you are praying.

I recently read a newspaper article about a popular attorney who is still practicing in his late eighties. When asked how he has managed to continue working so long, he replied that after his heart attack at age thirty, he resolved never to get angry again. He said that he withdraws mentally and often physically each time he feels he may be tempted to lose his temper. This is wise advice from someone who learned to control his emotional responses almost sixty years ago. Your mother's admonition to "count to ten" before reacting to the person who angers you was also good advice!

THE POWER OF FAITH AND HUMOR

Research indicates that people who pray and regularly attend a place of worship are healthier and happier than people who do not do these things. Medical research indicates that prayer helps coronary patients heal better and more quickly, even if the patients didn't know someone was praying for them. Some remarkable studies have demonstrated that plants are positively affected by prayer. There is definitely something special and powerful about prayer. Also, those who can forgive others release themselves of past hurts and move forward positively.[6] Learning to forgive others is a valuable tool for reducing stress and living positively. These extraordinary studies point to the reality that our thinking and our emotions have a profound effect on us and others.

Just as Solomon wrote generations ago, laughter truly is the best medicine! "A joyful heart is good medicine, but a broken spirit dries up the bones."[7] Now the research proves Solomon was right. Numerous studies have shown that some people can withstand tremendous stress, and they all have common personality traits. If you wish to be able to better handle stress, learn to use these common traits:

1. Care about others.
2. Have family and friends who support you.
3. Control difficult situations with humor.[8]

Dr. Jerry Wartgow was the best supervisor I ever worked for. Reflecting on his leadership traits, I recall that his wonderful use of humor made him so effective. As the executive director of the Colorado Community College System in the 1980s, Jerry had the difficult task of helping thirteen college presidents be successful with limited state resources. When we complained about the tough financial situation for operating our colleges, Jerry listened to the whining and ended up making a nonoffending joke about us, saying something humorous, or saying something self-effacing. The effect was always the same. We laughed and went on to the next issue, feeling pretty good about ourselves!

The brilliant thinker and writer James Allen stated, "There is no physician like a cheerful thought for dissipating the ills of the body; there is no comforter to compare with good will for dispersing the shadows of grief and sorrow. To live continually in thoughts of ill will, cynicism, suspicion, and envy, is to be confined to a self-made prison."[9] Being a positive person has wonderful benefits. Being cheerful and full of good humor truly is medicine for body and soul.

REACTIVE VERSUS PROACTIVE THINKING

Each of us is in a constant struggle of mind versus body, or morals versus immoral temptations. Our minds should master our bodies. If the desires of the body master our mind, we become a slave to those desires of the body. We have the power to stay healthy, but we can relinquish it if we begin worrying about our health or if we stay in a perpetual state of anxiety or negativity. Similarly we have this internal battle for whether our rational minds will rule our emotions. People who allow their emotions to drive their behavior will become slaves to their emotions. People who learn to step away from themselves and view their choices or responses rationally will achieve a sense of control that will help them achieve the career success they desire. But don't misunderstand; we cannot totally separate emotions from thoughts. Some emotions are productive, such as love, joy, and hope. The negative emotions, such as jealousy, anger, and greed, hold us back. The goal is to achieve a sense of self-control that will help you achieve your career goals by learning to think logically, harmoniously, and compassionately.

We will become either reactive thinkers or proactive thinkers. Reactive thinkers respond to external stimuli (their environment) and internal stimuli (their beliefs and emotions) without much rational thinking about them. Proactive thinkers will make a conscious effort to think rationally about every external and internal circumstance in order to make good decisions that will yield the outcomes they desire. Most of us are both reactive and proactive thinkers, but each of us has a dominant way of thinking. For example, when a dominantly reactive thinker receives an insult, his first reaction is to hurl one back at the person who made it. A proactive thinker will have anticipated the insult or will at least possess the self-control to analyze the situation before responding. In either case, he will have time to give proper thought to the situation and ignore the insult or respond by asking what caused the person to make such a statement. In this manner, the proactive thinker takes control of the situation, having a positive effect on the circumstance.

WHY DON'T WE GET WHAT WE WANT?

Mind is the Master-power that molds and makes,
And Man is Mind, and evermore he takes
The tool of Thought, and shaping what he wills,
Brings forth a thousand joys, a thousand Ills:—
He thinks in secret, and it comes to pass:
Environment is but his looking-glass.[10]

James Allen's poem captures the very nature of our world. The way we view the world is pretty much the way it will be for us. Our thoughts are reciprocal. What we send out is what we get back. If we view the world and others with suspicion, distrust, and low expectations, we will be perceived with suspicion, distrust, and low expectations. I agree with Dr. Wayne Dyer's quote: "You get treated in life the way you teach people to treat you."[11] This truth of reciprocity is so important to your success that I have devoted chapter 6 of this book to it. In the meantime, understand that you are treated as you treat others, and you tend to receive what you desire.

"You get treated in life the way you teach people to treat you."
—Dr. Wayne Dyer

Millions of people go through life primarily as spectators. They live vicariously, as passengers rather than as pilots. They let themselves become little more than reactors to circumstances, never realizing that they have the ability to control most of their circumstances. No doubt you have met some negative people. I know one in particular who was smart and had the ability to move high up in her career, but her habit of viewing everything as negative impeded her career. She was caught up in suspecting everyone was against her, and in the end, they generally were against her. In this egocentric behavior mode, she also tended to see life as all about herself rather than seeing life as integrated with others who were equally important. Rick Warren's book *The Purpose-Driven Life* gives advice to such self-centered people. His first line in chapter 1 is, "It's not about you."[12]

Indeed, until we learn to get beyond ourselves and control our feelings, we will continue to wonder why life isn't turning out as we want. Unfortunately some people employ chicanery or deceit, assuming that such behavior will give them an advantage over others. It may appear so at first, but such unsavory behavior will return only unsavory results. They have difficulty understanding that life is not about them. Life is about understanding that your Creator wants and expects you to lead a life with purpose, a life that serves Him and others.

To understand why you often don't get what you want, you must first understand that you can take control of your life. You should work to rise above the reaction mode of behavior to a more determined, intentional mode of behavior. You must learn that the power to envision a goal, develop a plan, and work that plan to achieve the goal is an opportunity for all of us. Everyone has the opportunity to get what he or she wants by seizing the unique power of thought. Of course, thought without the execution of the plan will have little chance of being successful. You must still sacrifice to obtain what you want. If you want a better relationship with someone, you must sacrifice some time to be with him and learn about his interests and goals. Then you should be willing to do things that interest him and help him achieve his goals. To get a new job, you must put in the time to research and develop a plan on how to obtain that job. But the most important point is to first learn that you can take more control of your life and thereby get more of the things you want.

Simply put, you can control your life by taking responsibility for it. If you don't take responsibility for your life, you will allow circumstances to control you. You will be acknowledging that you have relinquished the power to control your own life.

THE FEAR FACTOR

Two major causes behind not getting what you want are doubt and fear. Bear in mind that doubt and fear are emotional feelings and not rational thoughts. A fear response can be good if it keeps you from driving too fast on the highway or attempting something else that could result in injury. But let's examine how fear can keep you from getting what you want.

How many times have you wanted something, but your doubt about your ability to achieve it kept you from pursuing it? The base emotion behind doubt is the fear that you will fail at something. And heaven knows we can't fail at anything, because that would make us look bad to others or in some way negatively affect our self-esteem. That's the thing, then. We human beings have the unique ability to protect our pride by often behaving in insecure ways, including not taking significant risks. In this way we can maintain our self-esteem and stay proud of ourselves.

Self-pride is often created on the shaky foundation of insecurity. We're insecure because we are afraid that other people won't accept us or be impressed with us, or because we are afraid to fail at anything. The rational mind, by learning to think objectively and reasonably, is able to rise above its feelings of insecurity, pride, doubt, and fear and recognize that these things are basically childish, unimportant, and destructive.

It is difficult to ignore the basic feelings that we all have. However, with resolve and intentional thought, we can begin to recognize destructive feelings for what they are, and learn to ignore them. James Allen says that the will to take control of our feelings springs from the knowledge that we can control our feelings: "Doubt and fear are the great enemies of knowledge, and he who encourages them, who does not slay them, thwarts himself at every step. He who has conquered doubt and fear has conquered failure."[13]

People with successful careers learn to overcome insecure feelings by recognizing that insecurity is simply an emotion and does not represent their core being. They also understand the importance of continuing to grow as people and expand their sphere of influence. Once you stop growing and try to hold on to your career gains, you begin to slip backward, losing the very thing you've worked so hard to get, and your insecurities increase. So stay focused on growing in your career and as a person. Continue to set higher career goals, and you will be astonished at your achievements. Remember, the more you take career risks and succeed, the less insecurity you will encounter.

> Once you stop growing and try to hold on to your career gains, you begin to slip backward, losing the very thing you've worked so hard to get, and your insecurities increase.

To completely separate your feelings from your thinking process is probably unachievable and certainly unwise. To do so would mean to separate yourself from the company of others and from the ability to enjoy the social activities of your environment. Some monks and spiritual gurus have been attempting such things for years, and their results are impressive. But unless your career vision is to live alone and contemplate the meaning of life, I suggest that you simply work to understand and control the emotions that interfere with achieving your career goals.

Living a rational and healthy emotional life that puts others before you should be the goal. No one likes to work with someone, especially an aspiring leader, who wears his emotions on his shirtsleeves or thinks only about himself. Most career visions include leadership positions, and the most effective leaders have learned to think rationally, keep a sense of humor, and lead with a spirit of service to those whom they lead. Life would be very dull without the healthy integration of our rational and emotional selves.

CLOSE-MINDEDNESS AND DEFENSIVENESS

When confronted with the topics of close-mindedness and defensive behaviors, most of us abruptly respond by closing our minds and using our ego defenses to deny that we have them. Don't worry about it. If you are human, you undoubtedly have some close-mindedness and employ defensive maneuvers to maintain a reasonable modicum of self-esteem. It is probably healthy to have some of these characteristics. But when they get out of balance with rational thinking or interfere with your ability to achieve a goal, it is time to confront them objectively and appropriately modify their use. People with successful careers make it a habit to examine their behaviors and eliminate as much defensive behavior as possible.

Drs. Linda Elder and Richard Paul consider close-mindedness as a pathological disposition of the human mind. They suggest that we sometimes have egocentric memories that tend "to forget evidence and information that do not support our thinking and to remember evidence and information that do." We also have a tendency to see ourselves as the possessors of truth, and we can be egocentrically blinded by not noticing "facts and evidence that contradict our favored beliefs or values."[14]

Essentially we strongly protect our beliefs and values. This is not a bad thing, but when this protective behavior negatively affects our ability to reach our goals or to be rational persons, we should consider being more truthful with ourselves. The same is true when people put their complete trust and faith in another human being. Consider Jim Jones and the mass suicide in Guyana.

As a young man, I came to trust and believe in President Richard Nixon, particularly with his worldwide inclusion of China and his efforts at peace in Vietnam. I even wrote a college term paper about his ethos and his excellent diplomatic abilities. My professors didn't like him, but I came to admire this person who came from humble beginnings and by intelligence and determination garnered the most important job in the world. When Watergate surfaced and Nixon was dubbed a crook, I went into complete denial and blamed the whole thing on partisan politics. Not until I saw him leaving the White House in disgrace did I even consider the facts. It was a shock to discover my egocentric blindness, but I have continued to try to keep it to a minimum since that revelation.

We use all sorts of defensive behaviors to protect our beliefs and values and to get what we want. We become comfortable with our view of the world and our place in it, so it should be no surprise that we will maneuver to stay comfortable. Just as babies will do whatever they can to stay warm, clean, and well fed, adults will do whatever they can to stay psychologically comfortable.

Some common defense mechanisms, first identified by Sigmund and Anna Freud, include *denial, projection, rationalization, stereotyping,* and *scapegoating.* To go into denial is exactly what I did when I didn't want to believe President Nixon had a serious character flaw. Projection involves attributing one's personal flaws to another; for example, a husband accuses a wife of cheating when he is doing the cheating. We all rationalize from time to time, giving us the excuse for shortcomings, so we can avoid criticism. For example, the end justifies the means, doesn't it? Stereotyping is a dangerous self-deception that lumps people together based on some common characteristic, thereby forming a biased view of those people. The most common defensive maneuver at the workplace is scapegoating. This is used to protect oneself from criticism by blaming others or circumstances for one's faults or failures.[15]

Unfortunately most of us employ defensive mechanisms at times when we shouldn't. Over the years it just becomes a habit. It appears to me that all of us have an inner struggle between our values and our desires. We have a conflict of two natures. If we give in to the temptation to violate a belief or value, we will attempt to deceive ourselves by rationalizing or ignoring our disturbing behavior. Most incarcerated people will claim they are innocent or at least victims of overly harsh sentences. They can say this because they believe it. The power of rationalization is strong enough to change a person's sense of reality.

One of my most vivid memories as a three-year-old occurred when I faced a circumstance and allowed a selfish desire to overcome my sense of proper behavior. I loved to have my older brother, Bobby, read the Sunday funnies to me. It was a weekly ritual that after church and while dinner was being prepared, Bobby read all my favorite newspaper comic strips to me while I sat in his lap. On one particular day, Bobby was not getting to the funnies fast enough to suit me, so I ripped the paper from his hands and tore it in half. "Now no one can enjoy the funnies since you've ruined them" was Bobby's stern response. Even at that young age, I knew better than to exhibit such behavior, but I felt he deserved my anger because he was frustrating me by keeping me from what I wanted. People still frustrate me when they become barriers to what I want, but I've generally learned to control my reactions much better. I haven't torn a newspaper in years!

As we get older, we get subtler and cagier as we struggle, sometimes unconsciously, to get what we want, even though we compromise a belief or value. We have to use a defensive tactic to delude ourselves that we are not violating a personal belief or value. I am sure that Richard Nixon rationalized that stealing information from the competing political party was a smart and even fair thing to do. Otherwise, he would have to admit that he violated one of the Ten Commandments, and he couldn't do that because he had been religious all of his life.

We live with stereotyping in the news every day. If ever we need to rise above our prejudices and use our rational minds, it is now. Not all Muslims are terrorists; not all whites are prejudiced against African Americans; not all men think women are inferior. Stereotyping is a curse to humanity, and your chances of career success in this increasingly diverse world will be minimized if you employ this defensive mechanism.

Scapegoating is so common that it is almost accepted as normal behavior. As a leader, I continuously tell my subordinates not to worry about making mistakes; just learn from them and don't repeat them. Yet scapegoating frequently occurs. I was about to be fired from a job one time because my supervisor, a deputy chancellor, placed all the blame for a technical problem on me. I

stewed for two days until the big meeting was held with the college chancellor, where I was supposed to be dismissed. At the end
of his opening remarks, I made no excuses and did not use scapegoating; I accepted full responsibility for the problem. My
remarks astonished the deputy chancellor and befuddled the
chancellor. I kept my job and my self-worth, and my reputation
increased. No one is perfect, and no one expects you to be perfect.
Besides, often the best learning opportunities come from your
mistakes. Accept the fact that you are fallible, openly admit it, and
you will be happier and more respected by others.

There are still times that I, like most other humans (this is
bordering on scapegoating), will sometimes attempt to discredit
those who become barriers, thereby deceiving myself in justifying
my unfair behavior. Intellectually I know that such behavior is
discordant, but those darned emotions are difficult to ignore. In
the meantime I continue working on becoming a better proactive
thinker and a better person. Will I ever achieve perfection? Of
course not, but it is a worthy goal and a beneficial process to continuously work toward self-improvement.

LIFE IS WHAT YOU MAKE IT

The surest path to career success is by learning about and controlling your inner self. James Allen explains that the cause of all
power and all weakness is within us, and the secret to happiness,
or sadness, is also within. People who feel chained by their circumstances should look within for the keys to better circumstances. If
we wish for better opportunities and circumstances, we must learn
to create them. Allen states, "You may bring about that improved
condition in your outward life which you desire, if you will
unswervingly resolve to improve your inner life."[16] This reminds
me of a recent movie starring Morgan Freeman and Jim Carrey,

titled *Bruce Almighty*. Jim Carrey anguishes over the news that Morgan Freeman, who plays God, is leaving to go back to heaven. Carrey explains that Freeman (God) can't leave him because he won't know how to handle life's problems here on earth without him. Freeman replies, "That's the problem. Everybody has problems, and they keep looking up!" Freeman wasn't suggesting that man should live without God, but he was making the point that by looking within ourselves, we can help ourselves through most problems. Successful people learn to look to God and within themselves for answers, and they gain power by yielding to their spiritual consciences rather than their corporeal desires.

There is no guaranteed path to career success. But if you understand your motivations, are honest with yourself, follow moral values, and have confidence in yourself, you will be more likely to set a pathway to a successful career. As you become and stay mentally, spiritually, physically, and emotionally balanced, most things you seek naturally fall into place. When some aspect of your life gets out of balance, things you seek become more difficult to find.

Think about the clothes washer. It does a great job of washing clothes as long as everything is in balance. If it gets out of balance during the spin cycle, the machine will dance across the floor and shut itself down. We are like that washing machine. If our behaviors get out of balance with our beliefs and values or if we ignore one aspect of our mental, spiritual, physical, or emotional existence, we will spin out of control.

If you are working diligently to get what you desire, but aren't being successful, take an honest review of your inner self. Are you a positive person? Do you really expect to be successful? Do you take on new challenges with enthusiasm and a positive attitude? Or do you think things are stacked against you, and there is little use trying? Remember, life's circumstances will control you, or you will control life's circumstances. The choice is yours.

There are thousands of stories about people in this country who conquered seemingly insurmountable circumstances to become successful in the end. Consider George Washington, Booker T. Washington, Abraham Lincoln, and Helen Keller. Remember my students Kevin and James? The good news is that people are taking control of their lives and being more successful every day in this wonderful country that provides infinite opportunities. You can do the same thing. Your thoughts will ultimately determine your attitude and your altitude for success!

HOW TO GET WHAT YOU WANT

As simple as it may sound, people must want something before they get it. If you don't have a clear picture of your first career job, or the next one, you will not likely be successful. Set your personal vision, develop your plan, and execute the plan with vigor. As you connect and reconnect your thinking with your vision, dismiss unproductive or negative thoughts, stick to your purpose, believe you will accomplish your goal, and devote your energies toward achieving it. Your thoughts toward your career goal must have a purpose and be grounded in honesty and service to others.

WHAT SHOULD WE THINK ABOUT?

For generations, people have been wondering what to think about in order to have a good life. The apostle Paul told us what to think about:

> Be transformed by the renewing of your mind, so that you may prove what the will of God is, that which is good and acceptable and perfect. For through the grace given to me I say to everyone among you not to think more highly of himself than he ought

to think; but to think so as to have sound judgment, as God has allotted to each a measure of faith. (Rom. 12:2–3)

Finding your purpose and being in harmony with His purpose will produce a personal transformation and sound judgment. My purpose here is not to preach, but to briefly examine the wisdom of Scripture for your benefit.

In his letter to the Philippians, Paul was even more specific about the things that we should think about. He wrote, "Whatever is true, whatever is honorable, whatever is right, whatever is pure, whatever is lovely, whatever is of good repute, if there is any excellence and if anything worthy of praise, dwell on these things" (4:8).

EXERCISES FOR GETTING WHAT YOU WANT

One healthy exercise for getting what you want is to make a habit of self-examination. When something goes wrong, you are involved in a disagreement, or something appears to be taking too long to come to fruition, ask what you could have done differently to produce the desired or better results. If you are honest with yourself, this process of self-discovery will help you solve the problem and mature more at the same time. You should do this self-talk exercise often. As with most things, the more you do it, the easier it becomes, and you become more proficient at doing it.

Another healthy but sometimes uncomfortable activity for self-examination is to seek a 360-degree evaluation of yourself by your superiors, peers, and subordinates. This feedback can be rather revealing and quite helpful because the first step toward improvement is to know what needs to be improved. Some people advocate that you simply ask your family and friends for feedback on your behavior. I would discourage this since you will likely receive biased feedback at the least, and you might strain a relationship at the worst.

One of the best activities to help yourself achieve your goals is to identify your limitations relevant to your career. It is difficult to identify your limitations without the benefit of outside feedback. But if you are quiet and mentally review what you really know are your limitations, write them down. Follow up by reviewing your list of limitations, and determine which ones are self-imposed. There is no place for excuses in this activity. If you want to improve, you must be absolutely honest. The truth will reveal that most of your limitations are self-imposed by your beliefs. Now the question is, what will you do about them? How about developing a plan for releasing these limiting beliefs and following that plan?

I heard a wonderful sermon in which the preacher said the best way to avoid moral failure was not to put yourself in a position to be so tempted. If you have a weakness for abusing alcohol, don't go to bars or purchase alcohol. He had a good point. The best methods for us to avoid temptations, which limit our effectiveness, are to cease thinking about them, stay away from them, and ignore them when they present themselves. You will be successful by making the conscious choice to eliminate limiting behaviors and to replace them with facilitating behaviors. Each time you discover that you are hiding behind a self-imposed temptation or limitation, a warning flag should enter your conscious mind so you can consciously and deliberately cast that limiting thought away.

By the same token, mentally review your approach to doing things. Do you typically look for innovative approaches at work? Don't be afraid to be unconventional. You can learn to be a creative thinker by being with other creative thinkers. There is often a better way to accomplish something than the way it has always been done. The first step is to learn to think creatively. When facing some problem that demands creative thinking, try framing your questions in an unusual manner. For example, most businesspeople think about ways to beat their competition by asking themselves what things their competitors are doing well. This approach is logical, but the businessperson who also asks what he would do if he were competing with himself will find a better strategic advantage.

Faced with adversity, many people ask themselves what they have done to deserve such a problem. This victim syndrome leads only to more problems. It would be better to frame the question by asking what good can come from this adversity. Plywood was invented from a mistake. Tootsie Rolls were invented from a mistake. Penicillin was discovered from moldy bread. Tabasco was created from a few remaining pepper plants after the entire plantation was burned during the U.S. Civil War. Post-it Notes were made from glue that did not stick. Successful people always look for the bright side of a problem.

Creative people also persist in developing their ideas. Consider orthodontia. The braces exert just a little tension, but over time they move and straighten teeth in bone. I just read where Paul Moller, a California-based engineer, has developed a prototypical vehicle that is a flying car. Moller International has developed a feasible personal vertical takeoff and landing vehicle called the M400 Skycar. Moller has been using his imagination and his engineering skills to the optimum for forty years to achieve his dream.[17] Creative thinking is all around us, especially in our free market economy, and some astonishing things are happening. For example, some good thinkers at Cyberkinetics of Foxborough, Massachusetts, claim to have created a brain implant that may help people with motor impairments move a computer cursor just by thinking about it. The device is about the size of an aspirin and helps the brain translate thought into a computer. The first patient is already moving the cursor just through thought.[18] It appears that telepathic thought with an electronic implant is no longer a speculative idea. Now, this is creative thinking!

THE SUBCONSCIOUS

I do not intend to present a thorough discourse on the subconscious mind, but perceiving it as a tool will help you achieve career success. The conscious mind permits you to think, reason, analyze, calculate, and form judgments, among other things. The subconscious mind provides your intuition, inspiration, suggestion, imagination, and latent memory. Unlike your conscious mind, the subconscious is thought to be beyond space and time, embodying the knowledge of the past, present, and future. The subconscious is like a memory vault that records all your conscious thoughts and experiences and can use them to deduce solutions to problems, send and receive thoughts, or even help create a vision of the future. It can do this independently of conscious thought and seems to be connected to a broader knowledge base, often referred to as the universal knowledge or the universal mind. [19]

Some people suggest that all intuitive thoughts are from the subconscious, and that your sense of right and wrong, your conscience, also emanates from the subconscious. Whatever the case, it is without question that we all have some ability to tap into a source of knowledge greater than that of which our conscious minds are aware. Have you ever lost something, and when you least expect it, you remember where you left the item? Have you ever been working on a problem for days, and then the solution comes to you in a flash? These are common examples of the subconscious at work.

Most successful people learn to tune in to their subconscious by consciously feeding it problems, by thinking about them, and then being receptive to the subconscious when suggestions occur to their minds. Hundreds of inventors and writers point to the subconscious as the source of their creativity. When speaking of Henry Ford's success, his friend Thomas Edison said Ford used his subconscious mind.[20] Ralph Waldo Emerson is reputed to have written in his journals that he often wrote things revealed to him through his subconscious.[21] I can assure you that I believe my subconscious has helped me in my career and in my writing. I listen to it and use it as much as I can.

Robert Collier explained that we must not expect the subconscious, or the universal mind, to solve our problems or achieve our desires. He suggested we view this wonderful source of information and energy as we would a math problem. You wouldn't expect the math problem to be solved by the principle of mathematics. But by understanding and using the principle of mathematics, *you* could solve the problem. You must be the means for solving the problem by understanding and applying the principle that is available to you.[22] Being receptive to all sources of knowledge is a smart thing to do whether or not you understand how the sources work.

Many people have long believed that our thoughts send signals of some kind, most likely electrical or magnetic, that can be received by others or, in the Cyberkinetics case, by computer software. This unconventional belief has caused many people to be ridiculed by scientists and theologians alike. I suppose the first people who conceived the idea of transmitting voices and later pictures through the air felt similar criticism. I have a background in radio and television. These wonderful media work by converting sound and video into electrical impulses, which are transmitted through the air via the electromagnetic spectrum. These bits of energy are transmitted on a specific set of frequencies, or cycles per second, which can be received by a radio or television receiver that is tuned to those frequencies. If you want to watch Fox News, you will have to tune to the Fox News channel, which is assigned to a specific frequency. There are other energy vibrations all around us, but we must have the proper receivers and have them tuned to the proper frequency in order to interpret them.

Our limited receivers—our senses—can perceive only a very small portion of the electromagnetic spectrum, which is probably infinite. We can hear the things that radiate on frequencies that carry sound waves, and we can see light that radiates on the frequencies that carry light waves. But with proper equipment, we can perceive and even create X-rays, gamma rays, microwaves, and others that sixty years ago we knew nothing about. Since our thoughts emit electrical activity, who is to say that they aren't all connected on some range of frequencies that carry thought? Our thoughts are simply minute events of energy and information in a universe of energy and information.

The opportunity to achieve what we want rests in our ability to access the knowledge needed to be successful. Many people believe that the subconscious mind can change its sending and receiving frequencies as it needs to in order to access information that will help us with some problem or initiative. When you combine the possibility of having universal access of knowledge with the fact that our thoughts manifest themselves, the concept is illuminating to say the least! We really can create any condition in life that we choose; we really do have the capacity to be masters of our own destiny.

Many phenomena in our physical world can't be explained just yet. Remember the research on how prayer helps people to heal and even helps plants to grow? We have no concept of how to go about explaining them, we don't yet have the knowledge or technology to explain them, or we have not yet developed the realization that they even exist. My wife and I recently visited some dear friends, Phil and Pat Stanley, who live in historic Burkittsville, Maryland. One evening Phil drove us up South Mountain to Crampton's Gap, which was the site of a Civil War battle in 1862. Phil stopped the car on the downhill side of the gap, put it in neutral, and turned off the engine. To our surprise, the car began rolling backward and accelerating up the hill! Local lore suggests that the souls of the soldiers who lost their lives in the battle are behind the mystery. But for now, no one knows the cause of this phenomenon with any certainty. It is most likely a magnetic force that moved the automobile; nonetheless, the Stanleys and others who know about this curiosity take advantage of it to entertain guests. In the same way, we should take advantage of things that we don't completely understand, but that can be for our good.

You have no doubt encountered unexplainable incidents or know others whose dreams, vivid perceptions, or intuitions provided a precognitive experience, helped them solve some problem, or served as a warning of some kind. We often experience things that seem to defy our physical laws. Either they are physical and we don't yet understand them, or they are spiritual. In either case, you should use every tool available that will help you achieve your career vision.

Time and science will determine how thought travels and is received by others or even how thoughts become self-fulfilling by accessing other thoughts traveling in the universe. In the meantime, successful people recognize the power in eliminating negative thoughts and creatively accentuating positive thoughts. Remember, if it can be conceived and can be believed, it can be achieved. Use the current body of knowledge to help you solve a problem or create something, but don't limit your thinking because of it. The mind is like any other organ; the more you use it properly, the better it serves you.

USING THE POWER OF SUGGESTION

One of the most powerful tools for shaping beliefs is a suggestion made by others or one we make to ourselves. Repeated suggestions tend to become beliefs. Just like our beliefs, some suggestions facilitate our progress, and others limit it. Successful leaders understand the power of suggestion. Consider all the kings and queens in history whose trappings and absolute rule suggested they were superior and even had divine right to their thrones. Consider Saddam Hussein, who had his picture and slogans posted throughout Iraq to remind people who controlled them. Someone once said if you tell people something long enough, they will believe it. How else can we explain the attitudes of the Germans, Italians, and Japanese during World War II?

The best coaches know how to suggest winning thoughts into the minds of their players. Coach Herb Brooks, who led the 1980 U.S. Olympic hockey team to victory, convinced the players that they could beat the favored Russian team, or they couldn't have won. Look at how investors make decisions based on suggestion. Some forecaster suggests that the economy is expected to take a downturn, and people sell stocks like crazy. Consider hypnotists and how they use the power of suggestion for entertainment. The suggestions of others, whether negative or positive, can be very powerful.

Self-suggestion, often called autosuggestion, can be equally powerful. If you continue telling yourself you can solve a problem, and you come to believe it, you will solve the problem. The reverse is equally true. I have been blessed with the belief that I can do anything if I really want to do it. When I determine to do something, I go into it believing I will be successful. With this attitude, the battle is half over before I begin. Repeating thoughts via self-suggestion is effective, but only if you truly believe them. You must remove a deep doubt or fear about whether you can do something before you will truly believe that you will be successful.

My grandmother needlessly suffered from a negative suggestion all of her life. When I was about ten years old, I told her she was beautiful. She told me she wasn't really beautiful; she knew so because when she was a teenager walking with her sister, she overheard some boys talking. They were comparing the two sisters, and one said my grandmother's sister was the prettier one. I argued to the contrary as best I could, but Grandmother continued to believe she wasn't very pretty, all because of a fifty-year-old suggestion that became a lifelong belief. It is too bad that she didn't understand that other people's opinions do not necessarily represent the truth. Your opinion of yourself represents truth to you, so don't shortchange yourself.

> Your opinion of yourself represents truth to you, so don't shortchange yourself.

That little story also demonstrates the power of negative thinking. We know that negative thinking can affect us in many ways. You can spot someone who is thinking negatively just by his posture and facial expressions. Look at the mug shots of people who have been arrested, and you will see what I mean. Negative thinking affects people's health and ability to heal. Negative thinking will stymie your career growth because negative people attract negative people. Without the ability to develop strong relationships with positive people, you will be unsuccessful in achieving your career goals. Positive people can be spotted by their demeanor and facial expressions. Their optimistic words also give them away. Court these people as your friends. Negative people will send, repeat, and reinforce existing negative suggestions and beliefs, while positive people will do the opposite.

Are you familiar with the popular children's book written by Watty Piper, *The Little Engine That Could*? The best line was, "I think I can! I think I can!" For our purposes a better line would be, "I know I can! I know I can!" Suggest affirming thoughts to yourself each day. Visualize your short-term and long-term career goals each day. Recognize that you were created to win. Before you know it, you will have achieved them and will be setting even higher goals.

Visualizing your goal, developing and working on the plan, and reaffirming your ability to achieve your vision through positive thoughts still won't be enough to guarantee success. We live in a world where the association with other people is essential for career success. Those who become most successful in the world of work are those who have learned how to influence others in positive ways. The next chapter will provide you with the knowledge and techniques to become influential!

| LADDER-BUILDING TIPS |

1. Thoughts affect the body.
2. The subconscious mind is a useful tool.
3. Fear, self-doubt, and negativity will limit your success.
4. Only you are in control of your thoughts and emotions.
5. Believe in yourself; you were created to succeed!

| LADDER-BUILDING ACTIONS |

1. I recognize that the mind can do only what the body allows, and I am determined to take care of both by

_____

_____

_____

2. I recognize that my subconscious mind can be a helpful tool for achieving my goals, and I understand the power of positive self-suggestion. I intend to consciously think about my next career goal and will use the following self-suggestion to help me achieve it:

_____

_____

_____

| 5 |

THE POWER OF INFLUENCE

Service Above Self

Don't ask for power. Seek influence. It lasts longer.
—E. M. Forster

WE'RE IN THIS TOGETHER

Hermits can't accomplish much. Our world operates and improves only through the collective interactions of people. If you want to have a healthy, happy life and a successful career, you must learn to influence others. Successful people are good at influencing others to accomplish a desired goal. This is what leadership is all about: the ability to motivate others to achieve a common objective. You can have that dream career, but not by working in a vacuum. You must develop effective relationship-building skills and the ability to influence others.

The purpose of this chapter is to provide you with the time-tested and researched principles that will help you become a person of influence. This is the first major decision all successful professionals have to make. Do you wish to make a difference? If not, you will be unfulfilled. I know scores of wealthy people who worked hard all their lives to gain the material comforts and prestige they desired only to realize they are basically unfulfilled as human beings. Why? They are unfulfilled because they ignored the fact that they were created to care about and help others. It is not too late for them, however. They can always put their expertise to work for others by teaching, volunteering, and the like.

During your work life, will you focus on yourself or others? If you determine to focus entirely on your goals and desires while ignoring the interests of others, you will most likely fail and become insignificant. If you decide to focus entirely on others, you will be unjust to your family. The rational answer, and the one that most successful professionals follow, is to serve your family and others first and yourself second. In truth, as you develop a healthy focus on others, you will be helping yourself and your family also. Zig Ziglar has a belief that "you will get what you want out of life if you first help others get what they want." He is correct, of course. The greatest principle of salesmanship is to learn to give value first!

If you have determined that you do want to leave this world a little better than you found it, this chapter and the next will show you the pathway to realizing your dreams. Those who have successful careers will be the first to tell you that to get ahead, you have to get along. In other words, we live in a society where people are dependent upon each other. If you can't get along with people, your career will be stymied from the beginning. One of the best techniques for building meaningful relationships and getting along with people is to care about others. As you care about them, they will care about you. The golden rule about treating others as you would like to be treated is a universal law that is just as real as gravity.

I once worked with a man who was brilliant in his field of expertise. His only problem was that he couldn't accept other people's suggestions. It was "his way or no way." He never held a job for long. On another occasion, I worked for a man who delighted in making life miserable for his subordinates, thinking it lifted his prestige and reinforced his power. He was finally forced to retire, and he became a lonely person who probably never thought life was fair. Our interactions with others are reciprocal, and the sooner you learn this principle, the more successful you will become.

To be successful in today's work environment, you must understand how to prepare yourself to be influential with others. You can do this by developing a clear vision of what you want to become, getting the necessary knowledge and skills, and practicing the traits people seek most in their relationships. Are you fun to be around? Does a room light up when you enter it or when you leave it? Are you a good listener, or is it more important to always tell what you are doing? Can you keep secrets, or do you delight in demonstrating that you are "in the know" by telling others what you know? A good friend of mine often quips that he "can keep a secret; it's just those he tells them to who can't." Are you considerate of others, and do you care about them? These are some key attributes for developing good relationships. It is good to do a self-examination regarding your relationship-building skills on a regular basis.

Successful people also know how to leave the past behind them and look forward to their goals. They know that the best predictor of career success is to have a clear goal, a positive expectation to achieve it, and the self-discipline to continuously work toward it. As Benjamin Disraeli said, "The secret of success is constancy to purpose."

Unfortunately too many people do not realize that they have almost unlimited control over their lives. Some people, for instance, develop the misconception that they are inadequate, underskilled, or discriminated against in some way. These are excuses and defensive maneuvers designed to protect their egos.

This is typical but self-defeating behavior. If you feel inadequate, you should honestly identify why you think or feel this way. Then you should resolve to change how you think or correct whatever makes you feel inadequate. If you think you are under-skilled, acquire the training you need. Don't worry about the money; there are hundreds of financial aid programs for the needy. If you feel discriminated against, honestly examine each circumstance, and make sure you aren't simply reaffirming a core belief that you are being discriminated against. If you still think you are being discriminated against, confront in a professional manner the person or persons responsible, and work through it. Otherwise, ignore it. Those who fall into the trap of believing they are victims seldom become successful because they become too focused on themselves to do much good for others or themselves.

FOUR STEPS TO BECOMING INFLUENTIAL

People who learn to be self-confident have a tremendous advantage over people who struggle with confidence. Don't confuse self-confidence with egotism. Those who are confident in themselves don't have the need to show it. Those who are quietly confident in themselves and in their coworkers are the ones who have the potential to be the most influential and to get promoted to the top positions. Self-confident people cannot rise to the top, however, unless they learn to be persuasive and can lead people to be productive.

> Don't confuse self-confidence with egotism. Those who are confident in themselves don't have the need to show it. Those who are quietly confident in themselves and in their coworkers are the ones who have the potential to be the most influential.

There are four major steps toward learning to become influential:

1. Focus on the needs of others.
2. Do good things, and make a difference.
3. Employ the nine laws for becoming influential.
4. Learn to lead.

1. Become Influential by Focusing on the Needs of Others

Throughout our lives we are engaged in the selling process. If we aren't directly selling some product or service, we are selling our ideas and our personalities. Author Claude Bristol says, "As a matter of fact, all human relationships are based upon selling of one kind or another, and we all engage in it whenever we undertake to persuade others to our way of thinking."[1] Zig Ziglar, the most popular authority on sales, says selling is not a profession; it's a way of life. One of his favorite quotes is, "You've got to be before you can do and do before you can have!"[2] Yes, indeed, selling becomes part of what we do throughout life. If we want to influence people to accept our ideas or to follow us, we must first be the person we represent. If we truly care about others and their welfare, we will be able to influence them positively, and while helping them, we will be helping ourselves.

What is your purpose in life? The answer to this question is the key to your future. You might remember in Chapter 2 that I mentioned that you have to determine your life's purpose and then set a career vision that complements that purpose. We all have been given two great commandments, to love God and to love others. I hope that your determined purpose is congruent with these commandments. If it is, it is clear that you must spend much of your time on earth helping others. You might be thinking, *I don't mind helping others, but I'm not a salesperson and have no desire to be one.*

I have good news for you. You are already a person who sells, and you have been ever since you learned to get your way as a baby. The better news is that the best salespersons never think of themselves as selling something. They are simply helping people in some way.

How are you helping people? You generally help others by serving them in some way. I have been a member of the Rotary Club, a civic organization that serves its community, whose motto is, "They profit most who serve best." This motto sums up the entire notion of the reciprocal nature of service above self. You don't serve to get, however; you serve out of love and concern for others as a part of your purpose in life. You get good things from serving others because it is part of a natural law of reciprocity. If your motives are pure and ethical, good returns will be a typical consequence of your actions. The adage, often attributed to Winston Churchill, "We make a living by what we get, but we make a life by what we give," is as true now as it has always been. However, you don't have to keep your work life and your non–work life separate. In fact, it is preferable to tie the two together.

Separating your life's purpose from your work will create inner conflict that will result in an unfulfilled life and an unsuccessful career. Wise people recognize that if they are helping to accomplish their purpose through their work, life becomes ever so much more meaningful. Their work also becomes more fun. Truett Cathy, founder of the Chick-fil-A Company, puts it this way: "Learn to love your work and you'll never have to work again."[3] This is one of life's little secrets. When you work, remind yourself that you are working to accomplish your life's purpose. You will like working more, and your rewards will be more meaningful than just your paycheck!

One effective method for helping others is to listen to them. Many pastors and counselors have learned that it's not what they say to the bereaved or the sick that is important. What's important to people in these circumstances is that someone was there to listen to them. The sense of being affirmed as a worthwhile human being is significant to all of us.

The first step in any process of persuasion or influence is to build trusting relationships quickly. The best way to accomplish this social bond of trust is to make sure you listen to the other person and give him or her affirmative feedback. A positive nod or affirming phrases such as, "I agree with that," or "I see what you mean," will signal that you have heard and are paying attention to the other person.

You can also help to build trust with the other person by giving him your entire attention when talking with him. Look him in the eyes, mentally process what he is saying, and do not allow other things to distract you. I will never forget the first time my family and I met First Lady Barbara Bush. She flew to our city to be our college's commencement speaker. As we greeted her, she gave her undivided attention to each family member. Our twelve-year-old son later told us how much he liked her because "she made me feel important!" To be influential, we must believe that all people are important and, like Mrs. Bush, treat them accordingly.

Another Rotary Club motto is, "Service above self." When you begin to think about other people and put their needs above your own, you will have mastered a secret of leading a successful life and creating a rewarding career. I know a person whose charm and intellect have gotten him several high-level jobs. His grin is infectious, and he is great fun to be around. But his primary motive is self-promotion. He lost each one of those outstanding jobs because he never took the initiative to learn that by serving others, you serve yourself. Putting others first becomes a way of life, and others will appreciate you and support you because of it. The power of caring for others is tremendous. A well-placed phone call to someone who has been ill, a handwritten thank-you note to someone who has done you a kindness, and an invitation to lunch to someone who lost his or her job are simple examples of meaningful gestures that people appreciate.

2. Become Influential by Doing Good Things and Making a Difference

This is the simplest rule of all for becoming influential and achieving a successful career. If you do bad things, bad things will be your reward. If you aren't making a positive difference for others, what is the purpose in existing? The two activities complement and support each other. If you do good things for others, you will be making a difference, and vice versa. Doing good things will become second nature to you.

As mentioned before, researchers have evidence that the brain secretes certain chemicals that reinforce behavior repeated over a period of time. These chemicals provide a pleasing sensation every time we repeat the same good behavior. This chemical reinforcement leads us to form a habit, even an addiction, for doing those things because it makes us feel good physically. The unfortunate news is that the same is true for bad behavior. For instance, a person becomes addicted to gambling because his brain makes him feel good when gambling.

The brain is a powerful organ that, through its own thought, influences itself and the body it controls. Drs. John Spencer and Karen Shanor expressed this idea in the book *The Emerging Mind*:

Much clinical study has been devoted to demonstrating that the brain is able to control functions such as breathing, heart rate, and blood pressure, and even more specific areas such as cellular firing from various organs. And over the last few decades there has been an increasing recognition that the brain in fact is subject to the will of the individual. This is especially apparent with emotional attitudes, which can result from a

variety of sources including self-thoughts and personal interactions with other persons and the environment. Just as brain
chemicals can change thoughts, so too can thoughts change the
chemistry and functioning of the brain.[4]

There you have it. You can choose to do good things and
make a difference in others, and the chemicals in your brain will
reinforce this behavior. You will literally become addicted to
doing good things and rewarding yourself for those actions!

My friend Mark Erwin was the ambassador to the Mauritius
Islands in the late 1990s. He gives a great speech about his days in
Washington, D.C., just before receiving his appointment as an
ambassador. The founder and director of the National Prayer
Breakfast, Doug Coe, advised him to "do good" for the people of
Mauritius and for Americans. Longtime senator Jesse Helms
advised him to "make a difference for the world" through his
service as an ambassador. President Clinton told him to "have
fun!" Ambassador Erwin did all three and had a very successful
tenure serving the people of this country and those in the
Mauritius Islands. He tells me that those three recommendations
were uppermost in his mind as he went about his business every
day. Sounds like a good formula for successful living to me!

Will you always reap the fruit of your labors? Yes, but that
fruit is often unseasonably late. We don't always receive what we
hope for in the time that we want it. Patience is a virtue that is difficult for most of us to accept, but it does have its rewards.
Impatience raises your blood pressure, shakes the confidence that
others have in you, and generally makes you miserable. Learning
to be patient saves you from such misery. Continue doing what
you know is the right thing to do, and the difference you make
will bear fruit in time. Besides, just knowing you have done something good is a reward in itself.

> Will you always reap the fruit of your labors? Yes, but that fruit is often unseasonably late. We don't always receive what we hope for in the time that we want it.

You may wonder how you could make a difference in this world. Everything that has been created exists with everything else that has been created. There is a synergism among all things in the world, even thought. For every action there is a reaction, and for every cause there is an effect. You make a difference just by existing. You will never be fully aware of your influence on others and the conditions in which you live, but as you do good things, you will make a positive difference for others, yourself, and the condition of the world. A kind word may encourage someone to try harder or take a new risk to reach for remarkable achievements. That person may be the one who makes the next software breakthrough or becomes a beloved physician or a revered teacher.

A great way to make a difference is through your work. You will spend much time, thought, and energy in your career. People in the creative arts can make a difference by finding new ways to paint or perform. They will also make a difference in the lives of those who benefit from their work. People in the trades can make a difference in their craft by finding new or more efficient ways of doing things. They will also make a difference in the lives of those who benefit from their work. It doesn't matter whether you are in the creative arts, the trades, manufacturing, information technology, health care, or any other area of work. You can make a difference in your occupational field, in those with whom you work, and for those who benefit from your work.

Consider Thomas Edison, the most prolific inventor of the twentieth century. Do you think he made a difference in the people he touched and in the world? What about Mother Teresa? She established an order of nuns whose sole purpose is to give relief to the poor. These two people were not always famous, and it was not their goal to become famous, but you can be certain that they were always focused on doing good things and making a difference in their world.

It is easy to point out the differences that famous people have made, but rest assured that the guy next door or the woman who sits behind you in church may also be making a difference in his or her way. By using your unique talent, you will make a difference, especially if you focus on helping others. Ordinary people are making a difference every day, and so can you. George de Mestral from Switzerland is not well-known, but his invention of Velcro has been helping people around the world for decades. Candace Lightner is not well-known either, but the organization she founded in 1980 has made a colossal difference in the way we tolerate drunk drivers in this country. It is impossible to determine how many lives have been saved because of the work of her Mothers Against Drunk Driving organization.

I might never have written this book if Mrs. Scott hadn't planted a seed in my mind in 1954. I was about seven or eight years old and was playing with friends in front of her small house when she made a difference in my life. I was the seventh of eight children, and no one had ever attended college in my family. The elderly Mrs. Scott greeted my friends and me, and then asked me to come to her. I had never talked with her, although I'm sure she knew me. She said she wanted to give me something. She looked me in the eye and said, "You will be going to college someday, and I want to give you these coins to start your college fund." She then presented me with a handful of coins, probably under a dollar in value. The amount didn't matter. She believed in me and planted a powerful suggestion in my developing mind.

Each of us can make a difference in others and in our communities by simply seizing the opportunity to do good for others.

A kind smile, a word of encouragement, a helping hand, or a receptive ear can make all the difference in the world for someone in need.

3. Become Influential by Employing the Nine Laws for Becoming Influential

It should be noted that some of the material in this section is taken from a previous book I have written, *Nine Essential Laws for Becoming Influential.*[5]

I have known many influential people in my life, and all of them employed the nine characteristics you are about to learn. You can benefit from these laws for becoming influential by understanding them and putting them into practice as you work with other people. We tend to think that influential people are only those in higher positions of leadership or those who know and practice the art of selling. In truth, each of us can be influential if that is our desire. Your current position doesn't matter, nor does your personality type. It is true that leaders in high positions have the opportunity to more easily influence more people, and extroverts tend to influence more people because they have outgoing personalities. However, introverted people and those in lesser positions can also become very influential.

Thomas Jackson, often called Stonewall Jackson, was an introverted mathematics instructor at the Virginia Military Institute who showed no evidence of being able to lead men in battle at the beginning of the Civil War. Yet the shy teacher rose to become one of the most respected generals in that war. Nelson Mandela is a soft-spoken person who spent much of his adult life in prison, yet he became the president of South Africa. Consider Mother Teresa again. She had no high station in life and owned few possessions, yet she influenced the world by her acts of compassion. If you have a will to become influential, you will increase your influence when people trust you and your ideas.

We have entered a new period of work in America. Our global economy and our new technologies are causing jobs and occupational fields to change rapidly. People no longer expect to work for one firm for an entire career. In fact, smart workers view themselves as enterprises equipped with ever-growing skills. These independent, lifelong learners will contract their services to employers as long as they are happy and still growing in their chosen occupations and making progress toward their career goals. When they feel it is time to move up in their careers, they will try to do it with their existing employer, but will seek a new employer if necessary. Because of this need to sell themselves and their ideas to existing and new employers, they recognize the need to become influential.

A few years ago I conducted research to determine what attributes were most appreciated by employers. The idea was to identify the personal traits that influenced employers to hire and promote people. I surveyed chief operating officers and top human resources officers of large and small companies from a variety of occupational fields across the country. I then processed the data and discovered the nine common characteristics that all of the respondents identified as being important for people who were hired first and promoted most often. These nine factors for influence are listed in priority order. Note that all tend to be social and attitudinal in nature, which means that anyone can learn them.

> Smart workers view themselves as enterprises equipped with ever-growing skills. These independent, lifelong learners will contract their services to employers as long as they are happy and still growing in their chosen occupations and making progress toward their career goals.

1. The Law of Attitude
2. The Law of Communication
3. The Law of Work Ethic
4. The Law of Teamwork
5. The Law of Problem Solving
6. The Law of Results
7. The Law of Organization
8. The Law of Self-Confidence
9. The Law of Learning

1. The Law of Attitude. Enthusiasm is contagious!

Without a doubt, the most important attribute for becoming influential is a positive attitude. People love being around happy, positive, and enthusiastic people. Positive people attract others like a magnet. Who most influences you, positive or negative people? If you want to be like a magnet to others, resolve to become positive and enthusiastic about your work, the persons you work with, and life in general. And guess who has absolute control of your attitude? I am sure you guessed it right.

When you think about it, we don't have control of very much in this life. The two things that are within our control include what we choose to think about and how we choose to look at our circumstances. Certainly one affects the other. If we choose to think about the negative things in this world, our attitudes will become negative. If we choose to look at everything with a negative point of view, we will tend to think negatively. What we think about and how we perceive things are entirely up to us. Since life is too precious to waste on unproductive thinking and negative attitudes, it only makes sense that we resolve to think and act positively.

Look around you at the workplace. I will bet you can spot the rising stars with little difficulty. Are you perceived as a rising star? If you analyze those who are being promoted in your organization, you will see that they have positive attitudes about their work, about others, and about life.

Conversely you can also easily identify coworkers who are going nowhere. They complain and whine about almost everything, and they seem to relish discontent. Be careful about associating with these people. Remember that misery loves company, and they will warmly welcome you into their crowd, but only if you agree with them, thereby reinforcing their beliefs. In the process you will become negative without realizing it. Negative thinking, like positive thinking, can become addictive. The choice is yours.

People who continually seek sympathy from others are generally too busy losing to win. They don't realize that they have become their own worst enemy. Sometimes you can help someone develop a more positive perspective about his job or his life, but be careful that you aren't caught up in the web of dissatisfaction. Certainly we all face situations that produce anger, self-doubt, and disappointment, but it is important not to dwell on those things or they will become part of your character. Put them out of your thoughts as quickly as possible. Sometimes releasing a hurt or a betrayal is a daunting challenge, but holding on to it and nursing it are destructive. Pray about it, forgive those who have offended you, and move on.

But life's been unfair to me, you may be thinking. Welcome to the club! Life is full of unfairness, unhappiness, and negative circumstances. But they affect our attitudes only if we allow them to. We can complain all we want, but nothing will change those circumstances unless we resolve to change our attitudes about them through conscious

> People who continually seek sympathy from others are generally too busy losing to win. They don't realize that they have become their own worst enemy.

thought and action. Take control of your attitude, and remember that it is not what happens *to you* that is important, but it is what happens *in you* that matters. You will help control your destiny by controlling your attitude. By the way, life is neither fair nor unfair; life is what we choose to make it.

Only one person can decide how you will face each day. It is tempting to stay safely in the same job, avoiding the risk of failure, but you won't reach your career goals in this way. Learn to regard each risk and every adversity as an opportunity. Practice changing your attitude about things when you can't change the facts. Be creative and explore ways to advance your career, not by promoting yourself, but by helping people achieve good things and by being your best every day.

For twenty-six years, I have reminded myself to face each day with the positive attitude of the psalmist who wrote, "This is the day which the LORD has made; let us rejoice and be glad in it."[6] Choose something similar to mentally repeat every morning. I have a friend who has had a stellar career in the construction business. He told me that each morning when he inserts his key into his automobile ignition, he tells himself, "Okay, Bob, let's do something great today." Optimistic, cheerful people are happier, healthier, and get promoted more often than people who aren't optimistic or cheerful. The choice is simple, but it is helpful to remind yourself to be positive each day. To quote Ralph Waldo Emerson, "Write it on your heart that every day is the best day in the year."

2. The Law of Communication. Communicate well or forever be misunderstood!

Consider some of the most successful professionals you know. Without exception they will be good communicators. They may not all be great speakers or great writers, but they communicate well nonetheless. The ability to communicate effectively lies at the heart of leadership. If people can't understand you or you can't inspire others, your probability of getting into a position of leadership is severely restricted. If you can't communicate well, you won't be able to build relationships, which are what really matter to your career progress.

The old gibe that "people get promoted because of who they know, not what they know" is a defensive tactic used by people who don't know how to build good relationships. They obviously have not spent enough time on learning the communication skills necessary for building relationships. There is no dishonor whatsoever in getting a promotion because someone likes you and thinks you will do well in the new position. People hire people. People promote people. Be a people-oriented communicator, learn to build trusting relationships, and then you will be able to take advantage of this important law for career success.

People judge you in large measure by the way you communicate. People evaluate you by the way they see and hear you. If you insist on dressing as a nonconformist, people will rightly perceive you to be more concerned with yourself than the organization. If you fall into the habit of making snide remarks about others, people will rightly perceive you to be an unhappy person who feels the need to belittle others to boost yourself. In either situation, don't expect a promotion.

Supervisors hire and promote people who make a good impression, project confidence, and communicate well. Think about any meeting that involves free-flowing discussion. Inevitably the best communicators end up getting their ideas accepted by the group. It doesn't take people, especially supervisors, very long to recognize who the leaders are. The leaders are the effective communicators. Good communicators aren't always the people who dominate the discussion. Often the person who waits until last to summarize a discussion and offer his suggestions is the person whose ideas are accepted. Remember, God gave you two ears and one mouth. The ability to listen well is a valuable skill.

The ability to make effective and persuasive group presentations is becoming a fundamental part of personal career success. Most CEOs have learned how to present effectively. If you feel deficient in this area, take a course on public speaking or get someone to coach you, and put yourself in positions in which you will be required to make presentations. I have been speaking professionally for twenty years, and I am still learning about this exciting area of communication. Being prepared and learning to be yourself when speaking are the secrets to gaining the confidence needed to be a compelling presenter.

As in most situations, it's the little things that can derail you. The day-to-day interpersonal communication skills are extremely important. If you have grammatical or typing errors in your e-mails, people will note that you have a problem. If you consistently make grammatical errors when speaking, you will be judged as undereducated. If you constantly interrupt others, you will be lonely. Nonverbal body language can be an asset or a liability. If you say yes, but your body language says no, others will remember your body language.

I have interviewed hundreds of people as potential employees. If their cover letters or applications contain errors, they don't even make the short list. If they have good credentials and experience, but they lack the ability to represent themselves well in the interview, they are passed over. Interviews should be seen as exciting opportunities to sell yourself and your ability to add value to the organization, not something to fear or dread. If you fear or dread an interview, ask yourself what thoughts are producing such negativity. You should then dismiss those unproductive thoughts or change your perspective about the interview and

view it as opportunity. Some anxiety is normal and actually energizes you for the big event.

If you have a serious communication deficiency, don't lose
heart. Helen Keller could not see, hear, or talk clearly, yet she
graduated from Radcliffe and became an internationally famous
author and lecturer. Moses of Old Testament times had a speech
impediment, and his brother often spoke for him, but he over-
came his deficiency and led his people to the promised land.

Communicating effectively is an essential skill for becoming
influential. It begins with planning and ends with making a
great impression on paper, through electronic means, and in
day-to-day communication with others. It also involves learning
to listen attentively. If others don't think you are interested in
hearing their thoughts and ideas, they certainly won't be interested in yours.

3. The Law of Work Ethic. "Anything worth doing is worth
doing well!"

I can still hear my father's admonition that anything worth
doing was worth doing well, and his advice has been good for me
and my career. I hope that you remember some jewels of advice
that remind you to always do your best and uphold sound values,
especially at the workplace.

Our culture values general ethics and morals, which anyone
who hopes to be successful must believe in and employ in his or
her life. These generally accepted ethics are very much on the
mind of everyone these days, especially since recent incidents at
Enron, Arthur Andersen, and other corporations have demonstrated what happens when ethics are ignored. When you compromise your personal values or commonly accepted ethics, you
will suffer the consequences. When corporate officers compromise on ethics, the whole organization suffers the consequences.
Think of ethics as the foundation of your life and that of an

organization. If that foundation is compromised, fragile, and chipped away, it can no longer support you or the organization.

Human resources personnel are keen on asking interview questions that make the interviewee reveal his ethics. These situational questions usually place the interviewee in a hypothetical situation in which he must make a choice about an ethical dilemma. An even better question is to ask an interviewee to describe an ethical dilemma at work and how he solved it. Certainly every employer is interested in recruiting and retaining skilled employees, but all employers want employees who are honest, can reflect the principles of the organization, and possess good work habits.

Businesses exist to create wealth; therefore, they create products or provide services that must generate a profit. This profit is spread into the economy as the company compensates its employees, pays taxes, distributes bonuses, and spends money for expansion. Many people benefit from this wealth-producing enterprise. Workers and business owners are basically pursuing the same goal. Both want to better their condition by acquiring wealth. Smart people understand that company loyalty and high productivity will help them achieve their personal goals of improving their situation. Commitment and productive behavior are, in their simplest form, referred to as "work ethic." Since it takes committed and productive people to build and maintain a successful business, this is precisely what the marketplace rewards. Public-sector organizations in our culture reward the same work behaviors.

People and their collective ability to be productive drive our economy. The only way an organization can beat out its competitors and survive in this global marketplace is to out-produce or give better value and service than its competitors. People who adopt good work ethics become the most productive and inevitably rise to the top of their fields. American businesses are hungry for employees who show up to work on time, work a full day, have high integrity, take pride in their work, and go the extra mile for the good of the organization and its employees.

In today's economy you can depend upon this truth: if a society wants to live well, it must produce well. The same is true for you: if you wish to live well, you must gain skills and be productive. You see, it really is our collective ability to produce goods and services that provides the underpinning of America's economic health. The government does not drive the economy, and neither do corporations or businesses in general. This is why a good work ethic, which supports high productivity, is so important to employers.

Someone once said, "There is no traffic jam on the extra mile." Therein lies a golden opportunity for anyone who desires to have an extraordinary career. Develop excellent work habits, and always remember that a job worth doing is a job worth doing well!

> It really is our collective ability to produce goods and services that provides the underpinning of America's economic health. The government does not drive the economy, and neither do corporations or businesses in general.

4. *The Law of Teamwork*. "If you don't believe in cooperation, just observe what happens to a wagon when one wheel comes off."

That anonymous quote aptly describes the importance of teamwork. American organizations thrive on teamwork among their employees and teamwork with their suppliers and customers. We can increase our productivity if we work with others to accomplish some task or goal. Can you imagine a basketball player scoring any points against the other team if he didn't have help from his teammates? Teamwork has become a much-valued attribute in almost all professions.

In much of our early childhood, we are rewarded for individual performance. As we take our first steps, say our first words, and read our first books, we are the center of attention. Then some adult tells us to share toys or take turns with other children. This is a difficult but necessary lesson. If we can't learn to share and respect others, we will be at a disadvantage throughout our lives. Unfortunately there are plenty of adults who have to be the center of attention and have not yet learned the value of respecting others and sharing. It is unfortunate because there is little demand for people who can't work with others. Have you seen those two childrens T-shirts? One says, "Plays well with others," and the other says, "Runs with scissors." Which one are you?

As you seek your career goals, your reputation for being a congenial team player will become an asset. Your first task in any new job is to build relationships and demonstrate that you value working with others. The collective wisdom and creativity of teams are always better than those of just one person. Besides, you will learn much from others, especially in the first few months on a new job. Each contact with another worker is an opportunity to learn new knowledge or skills and an opportunity to make a new friend. Everything you do at the workplace should contribute to the common purpose of the organization and to your coworkers.

If you are not sure that you are perceived as a team player, simply reflect on your current work situation. Do people like you? Do they invite you to lunch? Do you share credit for accomplishments with others? Do you accept responsibility for problems? Your honest answers to these questions will give you a fair idea of how others perceive you.

Being a team player means contributing more than your fair share and being willing to consider other people's ideas, even when they make little sense to you. Keep an open mind to the ideas and thoughts of others. Maintain a sense of humor; humor breaks through uncomfortable moments, helps teams to bond together, and aids in the creative process. People who can laugh at themselves and with others are less rigid, are more willing to try new ideas, and are more often successful than people who are humorless.

The law of teamwork is fundamental to your success at becoming influential. Resolve now to talk less, listen more, criticize less, and praise more in every situation. You will feel better, and people will love you!

5. *The Law of Problem Solving.* "It is better to light a candle than to curse the darkness."

This ancient Chinese proverb perfectly captures the essence of solving problems. People are constantly on the lookout for others who can solve problems. By adopting this law as a work habit, you will have no problems becoming influential. People enjoy associating with visionaries, but those who have the ability to solve problems are more revered. We all prefer working with people who have the confidence, ability, and personal initiative to solve problems. It is easy to dodge responsibility by rationalizing that certain problems are not ours, but those who assume the responsibility to solve problems without being asked are those who move ahead in the organization.

If you want to have a successful career, meet challenges as they occur. Regard work challenges as opportunities to demonstrate your value to the organization. Don't just look for low-hanging fruit to pick. Those who take on serious problems end up learning the most about how to solve similar problems and are most appreciated by their peers and their supervisors. Consider young champion bull riders. They hope to draw the biggest and meanest bulls to ride. They are willing to risk being thrown off these bigger bulls because that is the way to earn the best scores. The same principle holds true at work. Don't be afraid of failure. Your supervisors will respect you and do everything possible to ensure your success. Tackle the big problems, and you will score big!

As a seasoned college president, I can spot problem solvers in my very first meeting with them. They have a real desire to contribute to the success of the organization, and they delight in taking on new challenges. They talk about solutions and opportunities rather than problems or potential problems. They are almost always optimistic, cheerful, cooperative, and customer focused.

If you want to become influential, you must become significant to those whom you wish to influence. If you want a promotion, you must become a leader figure to your peers and be recognized as such by your superiors. You become a leader by building trusting relationships, attacking problems, involving your peers, and celebrating your successes as a team. In essence, you become their coach, and each success elevates their self-esteem and their respect for you. Your significance in their lives increases with each success, especially if you give them credit for the successes.

To become influential, take the initiative when problems emerge. It is okay if it does not work out right the first time—or the second time, for that matter. The fact that you are willing to take the risk, to be the leader in a difficult situation, says volumes about you. George Washington risked his life by taking on the job of commander in chief of the Continental Army of the Revolution. He lost the first eight of nine major battles, but he won the one battle that counted.

Opportunities seldom come to us served on a platter; they are usually disguised as major problems. Problem solvers use their imaginations and ingenuity. They think outside the box and seek ideas from every source to help solve problems. They have maintained the childlike excitement of discovery. They are resourceful and clever about finding solutions to problems. Dr. Jonas Salk received the Presidential Medal of Freedom in 1977 for creating the polio vaccine at the University of Pittsburgh in 1953. Since then, this terrible disease, which killed or disabled hundreds of thousands of people, has been virtually eradicated. Dr. Salk used his creativity and all the resources and staff available to him to solve a problem for untold millions of people now and in the future.

> Opportunities seldom come to us served on a platter; they are usually disguised as major problems.

Not everyone will become as famous or affect as many people as Dr. Salk. But each one of us, by solving one problem at a time, is contributing to the betterment of our organizations, the people served by them, the economy, and ourselves. The residual benefits of solving problems make us significant to others and thereby influential. As we become more influential, our careers will soar.

6. *The Law of Results.* "Our grand business is not to see what lies dimly at a distance, but to do what lies clearly at hand."

This Thomas Carlyle quotation epitomizes the importance of producing results. Everyone, especially one in a leadership position, appreciates people who take the personal initiative to get things done. Research studies that attempt to identify the attributes most desired in leaders always list the ability to get results. Popular leaders are appreciated because of their ability to build and keep trusting relationships, but truly successful leaders do far more than become popular with their constituents. These leaders are successful because of their ability to get things done and to make things happen. They use their influence on others to accomplish the organization's goals.

Being results-oriented will make you a respected and much-sought-after employee, but don't confuse busyness with productivity. I have met hundreds of people who are busy at work, but never seem to accomplish anything. These people are more process-oriented than results-oriented. To avoid becoming process-oriented, put yourself in the mind of your chief executive officer, and consider what is most important to him or her. What things must be accomplished for the organization to reach its vision? Stay focused on accomplishing the things that really matter to the organization, and do less of the menial tasks that prevent you from achieving valuable results. I must remind myself to prioritize my work to ensure that I accomplish the important things first. It is very easy to get bogged down with phone calls, e-mails, snail mail, and meetings and never come to closure on the weightier tasks.

Each day as I drive to work, and for the first half hour at work, I organize my day. My schedule pretty much drives each day, so I am very careful about what is scheduled for me. My assistant screens my calls, my e-mails, and requests for meetings. Early in my career I attempted to please everyone and meet with anyone who wanted a meeting. This open-door philosophy sounds good, but is completely unreasonable. My stress level was sky high, and I scarcely had time to breathe, let alone plan for results. It is still a struggle, but today I drive my schedule rather than the reverse. I am happier and more productive, and so is my staff.

Results-oriented people thrive on accomplishing things, especially by working with others. They seek closure and enjoy finishing projects. Unfortunately they often become their own worst enemies by taking on too many projects at a time. In this instance, a time-management seminar can be helpful. Learn to do one thing at a time in priority order. Handle a piece of paper only once. Make your phone calls in one block of time. Leave some time between meetings to take care of unexpected tasks, process the information from the last meeting, or prepare for the next meeting. Don't receive an unscheduled visitor unless it's the boss, your spouse, or God.

I accomplish most tasks by working with a cabinet consisting of four vice presidents and my executive assistant. We recently were almost overwhelmed by work, especially since the demands for services have been increasing while budgets have been decreasing. We hired a facilitator and held a three-quarter-day retreat to address how to handle the increasing workload. We now categorize all of our action items as an *A* item that must be accomplished as soon as possible, a *B* item that needs attention within the next few weeks, or a *C* item that can wait. Just learning to recognize that not everything to be done is critical can save you much stress and keep you focused on the results that are most meaningful.

Everyone can find excuses for not getting things done. With a little effort, we can find any number of plausible excuses for not accomplishing something, and we can find plenty of company to verify the excuses. My advice is to be honest with yourself and refuse to listen to others who will help you rationalize why you couldn't or wouldn't accomplish something. When at work, avoid excuses as you avoid using profanity. Your reputation must be impeccable. You never know who talks to whom about you.

Life is often a balancing act. In getting results, remember to balance your zeal for results with the needs and interests of those who will help you get those results. People will remember what you have accomplished, but not how long it took to be accomplished. A leader who is all task-oriented and seldom people-oriented will soon be without followers. By the same token, a leader who is all people-oriented and seldom task-oriented will be replaced. A healthy balance of task and people orientation will yield the most productivity.

Take steps to avoid becoming overly process-oriented. Doing busywork and not accomplishing your assigned tasks is a sure sign that you've become process rather than results-oriented. When you or your team sets out to accomplish something, ask yourself whether doing it is in the best interest of your customers and your organization. If the answer for either is no, reassess your reasons for putting energy into that project, or dismiss it. Being process-oriented is generally unproductive and unbelievably bureaucratic. The Internal Revenue Service is an example of process orientation at its worst. The IRS code of regulations contains more than seven million words, most of which are left up to interpretation! Don't confuse busyness with productivity or process with results. Develop a bias for spending your time in pursuit of meaningful results.

> Don't confuse busyness with productivity or process with results. Develop a bias for spending your time in pursuit of meaningful results.

7. *The Law of Organization.* "Order is light, peace, inner freedom, self-determination: It is power."

Henri Frederic Amiel couldn't have said it better. Staying organized is a learned behavior. When you aren't organized, life becomes stressful, and both you and your career suffer.

Have you ever felt as though you were spinning your wheels and not really accomplishing very much? If you haven't felt like this, you are truly unusual. Everyone has days when things just don't quite fit together. In spite of these inevitable days of frustration, influential people always seem to find a way of getting the job done. They are able to move forward because they have the discipline to stop their busyness and reorganize their thinking and their priorities. They get themselves "squared away," as my Marine Corps friends would say. The next time you feel yourself spinning off target or are overstressed, find a quiet place, take a few deep breaths, and visualize yourself in a peaceful setting. After you feel your anxiety has decreased to an acceptable level, reassess your priorities for the day, and work only on them, one at a time. Avoid distractions, including mental and emotional distractions, as if they were the plague.

The following is a simple formula for being organized and staying in control of your work:

- Clearly understand the mission and vision of the organization.
- Prioritize your goals and tasks to achieve them.
- Do only one thing at a time.
- Evaluate your work for continuous improvement.

Being organized mentally is more important than being organized physically. You must also learn to think rationally, generally setting aside strong feelings and emotions. It is not desirable to completely ignore your emotions, but you must be careful that they do not contaminate your objectivity. Neither should you ignore your intuition. Your intuition is often valuable for making choices, but be sure you have looked at a situation logically and from a variety of perspectives before making a decision. Someone once said we should follow our gut instincts because these instincts don't doubt themselves. In any event, organized people usually view situations logically, from many dimensions, and temper their decisions with their instincts. They use a blend of thoughts, emotions, and past experiences to help them make decisions.

Successful people have learned to stay organized by using memory aids. If you try to remember too many things, you will forget some of them. I write myself notes throughout the day and night. I record them if I am driving, or I ask my assistant to put a written list of reminders on my desk to be ready when I return to the office. I can then dismiss those thoughts and relieve the anxiety of possibly forgetting something. More important, I can spend my mental energy on more productive thinking than constantly reminding myself not to forget something.

You should also practice thinking logically so that coworkers can follow your thinking. To be of influence, you should learn to frame problems or projects in a way that can be clearly understood. Without consistent and logical thinking, your peers and subordinates will be confused. I am so results-oriented that everything seems to be a priority and has urgency to it. This situation confuses people because they sometimes don't know how to prioritize situations that I ask them to handle. Fortunately, I am getting better at labeling our challenges or projects as *A, B,* or *C* in priority.

Being physically organized at work is a worthwhile goal. Your desk should be clear of everything except your mail trays and the current project on which you are working. You should understand the filing system and know how to operate the machines and technology necessary to do your work. There is nothing more frustrating than not knowing how to find something or not being able to use the technology to complete a task. Of course, it helps to have a competent secretary or administrative assistant!

Influential people understand that when it comes to quality, there is no finish line. These valued people regularly evaluate their goals and their work in order to improve. They continuously assess their work, including that of their subordinates, to determine how things can be improved. They recognize that key performance measures can be very helpful for evaluating priorities of the future. Being able to complete tasks and accomplish goals is much valued by the organization, but evaluating performance for continued improvement is the mark of a fully organized person.

8. The Law of Self-Confidence. "Early impressions are hard to eradicate from the mind."

Saint Jerome certainly stated a human truth. First impressions are lasting impressions. I once visited a job-placement department of a private college. A full-length mirror was placed at the entrance with a sign that read, "Would you hire this person?" It was an effective message to anyone who was seeking a job. People treat us as they perceive us.

The first sixty seconds of an encounter with a stranger are the most lasting. There is much truth to the adage that you never get a second chance to make a first impression. We exist in a world where our social experiences form the way we perceive others. If I encounter someone with tattoos and body piercing, I form an instant opinion. If I see someone who is well dressed and groomed, I also form an instant opinion. My opinions will be reinforced or altered after I visit with each person, but that first impression is powerful.

Your objective is to sell yourself and your abilities to others on a daily basis. Sell yourself not by becoming egotistical or taking credit for every accomplishment, but by giving your best every day and by projecting self-confidence. View yourself as an enterprise and the people you meet as your customers or potential customers. In this way, you will be focused on others and interested in serving them rather than yourself. By serving others, you will be helping yourself. Put your best foot forward, especially in the first sixty seconds when you meet someone.

Every social contact is notable. You never know who will be the next person of significance to your career. As I mentioned earlier, I often hear people complain that "it's not what you know, but who you know that counts." This is true! Now that you know it, use it. As you pursue your dream career, you should network with anyone and everyone. There is no end to networking. Life is about interactions with other people. Meet people with confidence, and let them know your career aspirations. Most people will want to help you if they know your goals. Don't forget the power of personal notes.

I always wanted to meet Zig Ziglar after I read his best seller

See You at the Top (Thomas Nelson Publishers, 1992). Years went by, but I never had a chance to meet this remarkable man. One day in 1987 I met a retired navy captain who told me about a Total Quality Management conference he was putting together in Colorado Springs. I was delighted to discover that he had booked Zig Ziglar as a keynote speaker, and I told him about my interest in meeting Zig. Not only did I have the opportunity to meet Zig, but I was seated next to him at lunch. We became great friends, and I served for several years on his corporate board. Zig even introduced me to Thomas Nelson Publishers, and this book is my third publication with the company. See how it works?

Sometimes you bump into someone who can help you by accident, but most successes come by intention. Make a list of people who can help you in your career. Determine how you can best get to know them, what value you can be to them, and then execute your plan with confidence and ask for their support. When I made my first application to be president of a college, I approached the process with much planning. I learned as much as I possibly could about each trustee and his or her family, including hobbies and interests. I also learned who their best friends were. I made a list of the community's key leaders and power brokers. I spent untold hours meeting the friends of the college trustees, the community leaders, and the power brokers behind their success. To each of them, I explained who I was and asked them where they thought the college should be headed to better serve the community. After listening to them, I explained why I wanted the job and what I could do for the college and the community. I then asked for their support. I got the job.

People who project confidence are people of influence. My wife and I had to purchase a new artificial Christmas tree this past year. We know very little about Christmas trees, so we were dependent upon salespeople to help us make the right choice.

The first two attempts to purchase a tree were a bust. No salesperson knew anything about the trees at the first store. The second store had someone who knew how to read the tree descriptions on the price card, but could offer no other information. At the third store, we found an enthusiastic saleswoman who confidently told us more than we ever wanted to know about Christmas trees. More important, she helped us think through the best size and type of tree for our purpose and how and where it should be stored after Christmas. We bought a tree from her.

Self-esteem projects itself in our demeanor, our dress, our posture, our facial expressions, and our speech. Everyone will be more impressed and influenced by the person who exhibits healthy self-confidence than someone who appears to be timid or less than confident. Would you purchase an automobile or a house from someone who lacked confidence? Would you promote someone who lacked confidence? The point is clear.

If you lack the confidence you know you need for progressing in your career, you can change the situation. Think honestly about what is driving your lack of confidence, and write those things down. Generally it is the lack of a credential or the lack of preparation that generates personal anxiety. Both can be corrected by gaining the credential or taking the time to prepare. Practice your ideas or your sales pitch on friends, and seek their feedback. The more you practice, the more confident you will become. If you are suffering from the way some adult criticized you when you were young, dismiss it. Each day is a day for new opportunities to improve, and the most important opinion of all is your own.

To be successful in a career, you must learn to feel good about yourself, your abilities, and your relationship to others. Your perceptions about yourself set the limits for what you can or cannot do. Self-esteem is the opinion you have of yourself, based on your attitudes toward the following:

- Your appearance
- Your physical abilities
- How well you did in school (perceived intelligence)
- Your confidence in social situations
- How you regard yourself[7]

Besides gaining the knowledge and preparation for a task to increase your confidence, the most important thing you can do is to build yourself up with positive words and thoughts. When you catch yourself saying negative things about your abilities, reverse your thinking and your words. Think about the successes you have already had, not about things that went wrong or might go wrong. Talk about yourself with confidence, not with put-downs. You will become what you tell yourself you can become!

9. *The Law of Learning.* "The education of a man is never completed until he dies."

General Robert E. Lee epitomized his own statement by continuing to learn throughout his life. Even after his distinguished, but ultimately unsuccessful, military career, he became president of Washington College, later named Washington-Lee University.

Learning has become a lifelong necessity. People who choose not to continue learning will be unsuccessful in reaching their full potential. The American marketplace is changing rapidly, and the academic, technical, and social skills required for people in all career fields demand continuous learning. Your willingness to gain new knowledge and skills represents the law of learning and will determine the success of your career.

As a young boy in the 1950s, I was curious about why our neighbor, a grizzled and reclusive old man we called Fuzzy, was so poor. "Old Fuzzy has a rough way of it, son," my father explained. "You see, he used to be a well digger, but modern technology came along, and he didn't keep up with it, so he was pushed out of a job." That moment made a lasting impression on me. If anything, the pace of change today is occurring at lightning speed compared to the changes in the fifties. We no longer live in a predictable world where we can expect to progress in a career based on the knowledge and skills we learned as young people. Just as poor Fuzzy pushed himself out of a job by not learning new skills, today's workers are suffering the same fate with greater frequency.

In North Carolina, we are busy retraining textile workers, furniture makers, and tobacco farmers. Those who are willing to gain the knowledge and skills to transition into the new jobs of the twenty-first century will do well. Those who refuse to learn new skills will likely increase the welfare rolls. But even if you are not laid off, you must stay current with the new changes in your field. Regularly read trade magazines, and talk about new concepts and ideas with your peers. The opportunity to learn new information and skills has never been better. The Internet makes learning accessible to everyone. Community colleges are convenient to most everyone, and many organizations provide professional development opportunities for their employees. Take advantage of every opportunity to learn more about your career field. When your superiors learn about your interest in learning, you'll have one more credit on the right side of the ledger.

If you think you have a knowledge or skills deficiency, you probably do. Identify it, and take steps to correct it. There is no shame in lacking knowledge or skills, but there is if you don't do something about it. Many famous people have overcome serious deficiencies to be among the best in their fields. Winston Churchill held the lowest academic rank in his elementary school. General George Patton was dyslexic and flunked mathematics at the U.S. Military Academy. Walt Disney was once fired because he had no good ideas! You get the point.

Many famous people have overcome serious deficiencies to be among the best in their fields. Winston Churchill held the lowest academic rank in his elementary school. General George Patton was dyslexic and flunked mathematics at the U.S. Military Academy. Walt Disney was once fired because he had no good ideas!

Think about these nine laws for becoming influential. Practice becoming adept at using them well, and you will become a person of influence.

By diligently learning and applying the power of influence, you will soar to the top of your profession. You have every reason to feel secure about your personal vision and your ability to achieve it. You were made to do great things, and you are bound only by your lack of belief in yourself. Once you recognize and claim the powers of vision, thought, and influence, you can be free from the gripping fear of failure. You will also cease being emotionally dependent upon others, and you will evolve into the person and the position you most desire. But hold on. It is the power of reciprocity that will elevate you as high as you want to go in life and in your career. Chapter 6 describes this wonderful principle so you can use it in your arsenal for success!

| LADDER-BUILDING TIPS |

1. Focus on the needs of others.
2. Learn to build trusting relationships.
3. Do good things.
4. Make a difference.
5. Practice the nine laws for becoming influential.

| LADDER-BUILDING ACTIONS |

1. I wish to make a difference in this world by

_____

_____

_____

2. I will build better relationships by

_____

_____

_____

3. The main barriers to reaching my career vision are

_____

_____

_____

4. I will eliminate these barriers by

_____

_____

_____

5. The most important law for becoming influential is

_____

_____

_____

| 6 |

THE POWER OF RECIPROCITY

We Reap What We Sow

We're rich because of our generosity, not the reverse.
—Dr. Claire Gaudiani

The principle of reciprocity simply means that we reap what we sow. It is a universal law that has been expressed in nearly every religion. The Bible refers to it scores of times, but never more plainly than in the apostle Paul's second letter to the Corinthians, when he said, "He who sows sparingly will also reap sparingly, and he who sows bountifully will also reap bountifully."[1]

THE LAWS THAT AFFECT US

The physical laws of this world are unbending, consistent, and applicable to everyone without exception. We cannot escape the influence of these laws. We can learn to use these physical laws for our advantage or disadvantage, but we will live with them as an ever-present influence on us.

If we step off a ladder, gravity will cause us to fall to the ground. If we fly on an airplane, we have the illusion of defying gravity when, in fact, gravity is still at work, or the airplane wouldn't have to expend energy to defy it. Eventually the airplane must come back to earth because of gravity. We see light because of the sun or some other energy source that produces light waves. Where there is no light, we experience darkness. There is no in between. There is either light or the absence of it. We can use light or darkness to our advantage or disadvantage.

All physical matter consists of atomic matter; each atom is made up of a nucleus and electrons. Even these smallest bits of matter are subject to the laws that affect them. We have learned to harness the power of electricity, but we could not do it without the consistently applied laws of power, resistance, and amperage. Once we understand our physical laws, we are capable of learning to use them for our purposes and for our advantage. But these physical laws remain just the same. If we attempt to violate these laws, we will suffer the consequences. My father-in-law was a master electrician, but he would tell you never to think of electricity as your friend. Yes, it brings us much bodily comfort, but if you use it in the wrong way, it can burn your house down, electrocute you, or produce any number of negative consequences.

We also live in a world of nonphysical or spiritual laws. These laws are just as real and have the same potential for good or harm as the physical laws. If we violate our personal code of ethics, we create personal guilt and stress. If we think negative thoughts, we will become negative-minded persons, and our health and happiness will be negatively affected. If we follow our code of ethics, we gain confidence and feel good about ourselves. If we think positively, we will become positive persons and will be happier and healthier. We can rationalize a bad deed by convincing ourselves that the end justifies the means or by using some other excuse, but we will have violated our code of ethics nonetheless, and our consciences will not allow it to be forgotten. Our self-esteem will be negatively affected, and we will suffer for it at one time or another.

If you go through life thinking only about yourself, you will miss the wonderful benefits that come from helping others. Egocentric people are generally absorbed with themselves and basically unhappy. Those who learn to serve others are focused on the bigger things of life, are better balanced, and are happier people. As you help others, help comes back to you. As you help only yourself, not much help from others will come your way. You really do reap what you sow.

Some scientists believe and are trying to prove that all laws and all things we experience are physical. They postulate that the brain is physical; therefore, the mind must be physical. We know that thoughts produce electrochemical responses and use up energy, so perhaps everything is physical. How, then, do we explain love? Our purpose here is not to debate whether all laws have a physical basis or whether they have been designed by God, but to demonstrate that we are affected by a set of physical laws and spiritual truths that cannot be denied or ignored. The more you learn to use these laws, the better you will be able to accomplish your life's goals.

The fundamental point in this discussion is to understand that you have the power to determine how you will use these laws. Obviously you will obey the physical laws, or you could die. You will also use these laws to your advantage whenever possible. But you must also determine how you will use the spiritual laws to your advantage. By the way, to ignore them is to court disaster. If you ignore the law of truth, you will be recognized as a liar and a deceitful person. How you choose to use these laws can make you or break you.

I believe the most powerful spiritual law for helping you get the career of your dreams is the law of reciprocity. Simply put, this is the law of cause and effect. For every action there is a reaction, but it is not an opposite reaction. As you do some kindness for another person, a kindness will, in time, be returned. Robert Collier believed that life is like mathematics. What you give on one side of the equation is matched on the other. Collier also had a prescription for life that is worthy of being repeated:

1. Find some worthy way in which God can express Himself through you.
2. Put your faith in Him, not in yourself or your friends.
3. Get above your troubles.
4. Imagine (visualize) doing what you dream about.
5. Work for your health in the same way.
6. Use your total intelligence; set high goals for yourself.
7. Learn to forgive.[2]

Anyone who aspires to have a successful career can put Collier's prescription to good use. He understood the principle and the power of reciprocity.

UNDERSTAND AND PROSPER

Do you remember being told as a child to do unto others what you would have them do unto you? That is the golden rule. It actually comes from a biblical statement found in Luke 6:31. This universal truth is not just something we use to help children understand how to get along with others. It is a truth that affects us throughout our lives. If you want people at work to treat you with respect and support your efforts to grow professionally, you have to treat people with respect and support them in their efforts to improve their careers. It really is that simple.

Please note that you have to make the first move. You have to give value to others first. Good salespeople know that they have to give value first. People have a tendency to return what is given.

If a salesperson helps a potential customer, it is much easier to make the sale because that person feels a sense of obligation to the salesperson. When I raise money for our college, I never ask for a donation until the college or I have rendered some value to the potential donor.

A few years ago a friend introduced me to a wealthy businessman. After the usual pleasantries, the businessman asked how he could help me and our college. I believe I could have gotten a respectable pledge from him at that moment. Instead of making a pitch for a donation, I suggested that the better question was, how could I help him? I explained about our expertise in customized training for businesses and asked if his retail store employees needed any training. That conversation resulted in a wonderful relationship between the college and his corporation, and the college has been training his employees ever since. A year after our first meeting, I invited the same businessman to one of our campuses and reviewed how the college had helped his company and suggested a way in which he could help the college. This generous donor gave us several million dollars for a student scholarship endowment. Make it a practice to give value first; it works wonders!

People have a natural urge to reciprocate if someone does them a kindness. My wife and I gave our new neighbors a small gift for Christmas a few years ago. The next day we received a gift basket worth three or four times the gift we gave them. I have been trying to even the gift since that time.

By the same token, people have the urge to reciprocate if done a disservice. If someone is betrayed, he seeks revenge. The first time another boy hit me in elementary school, I hit him back. As successful people age, they learn to control their vengeance but become very generous in giving value to others. We have this built-in sense of justice that compels us to help others, and that translates into the principle of reciprocity. You can use this principle to your great advantage when networking for a job or when building relationships at work. Giving credit to others, writing congratulatory notes, or buying someone's lunch will produce positive returns and help your career. Yet you learn to help others not because of an expected reciprocation, but because it is the right thing to do.

The old saying "what goes around, comes around" is true. If you sow dissension and divisiveness, sooner or later you will find yourself in the middle of the same. If you spread kindness, you will be treated kindly. As children, most of us thought we could violate some rule our parents gave us and not be found out. In truth, we never got by with anything, even if our parents didn't discover our infraction. Our consciences scolded us worse than our parents could. If I allow it, my conscience will still grate me for things I regretfully did as a young man. This principle is just as true today as when you were a child. Fortunately as adults we're better equipped to think through the morality and the probable consequences of an action before committing it, and we have learned to leave the past in the past and move forward with confidence in doing good for others.

CULTIVATE YOUR GOALS

Life has often been compared to gardening. If you want tomatoes, you prepare the soil and plant tomato seeds or plants. If you want carrots, you plant carrot seeds. We don't plant squash seeds and expect watermelons to grow. The gardener also knows that weeds and bugs can enter the garden and ruin the plants. He anticipates these invasions as part of gardening and takes steps to prevent them from overwhelming his crops. He faithfully pulls weeds, fertilizes the soil, and sprays the plants to eliminate the bugs. In due time, the gardener reaps the harvest exactly as he sowed it.

Like a garden, every thought and goal is a seed that begins to germinate in our lives. If you nurture them and continue to support them, they will manifest themselves exactly as you envisioned. Once you set your vision for your dream career and develop a plan to reach it, you must stay focused and continue to work the plan. You will have challenges and encounter barriers along the way, but by cultivating the goal and eliminating destructive thoughts and actions, you will harvest what you have sown.

Remember that not all seeds germinate and produce a harvest quickly. The radish plant will begin growing a day or so after planted and will produce the first vegetable in the garden. Tomatoes take weeks to produce fruit. The grapevine takes years to produce fruit. Not all of your goals will come to fruition as quickly as you might like, but they will eventually come to pass if you continue to support them and nurture them in an environment where they can grow.

My wife and I once visited Hovenweep, an ancient Anasazi village just outside Cortez, Colorado. We were astonished to see a garden of beans, squash, and blue corn that had originally come from six-hundred-year-old seeds and beans found in one of the cliff dwellings. Like seeds, thoughts and goals have latent power that can yield results if properly nurtured.

STAY FOCUSED

It is easy to get distracted from our goals. Marriage, children, illness, peer pressure, and any number of issues can divert us from our career goals, but those who learn to balance life and focus on one thing at a time will achieve their goals. A wise person once said, "If you chase two rabbits, both will escape."

The 2004 Bassmaster Classic tournament was held at Lake

Wylie where I live in North Carolina. It was an exciting three-day national tournament in which sixty professional fishermen competed for the grand prize of $200,000 and the title of Bassmaster Classic champion of the year. The leading fishermen changed each day, and it was anyone's guess who would be the big winner. In the end, the fisherman who stayed focused on his goal won the tournament. Takahiro Omori grew up in Japan, and in his teenage years he determined that he was going to become a professional bass fisherman. His dream goal was to win the Bassmaster Classic. Armed with his career dream and little else, Omori came to America in 1992. He did not speak English, had no job, and for a number of years barely made a living. He didn't win a tournament until 1996.

Then eight years later, Omori was fishing in his dream tournament at Lake Wylie. In the last five minutes of the third day, he stayed focused and caught two fish weighing a total of three pounds. He made it to the weigh-in on time and won the championship by about three pounds. If Omori had allowed defeating thoughts to limit his concentration, he likely would have missed catching those two winning fish or would not have fished until the last possible minute. Staying focused pays off!

WATCH YOUR MOTIVES

Some sociologists insist that there is no such thing as altruism, that people don't help others out of the goodness of their hearts. According to their reasoning, people help others because it makes them feel good; therefore, they help others out of selfish reasons. If that's true, so what? I choose to believe that there is goodness in people and that their good deeds should be rewarded. If they weren't rewarded by feeling good about themselves or receiving something in return, the principle of reciprocity would not exist.

But it does exist, and we should use it for all the power it is worth to us.

It is good advice to review your motives in helping others. Like a boomerang, our thoughts and actions will return to us, whether those thoughts and actions are good or evil. But if you hope to achieve your career goals and lead a happy and fulfilling life, you must resolve to sow good deeds. My experience has been that people who care only about themselves and leave carnage in their climb to the top of their career ladder are standing on a cracked rung. They may reach some remarkable heights in their selfish climb to the top, but they do not stay there long. They have failed to understand that their thoughts and motives became the architecture for their success or lack of it. If you build your success upon dishonesty and selfishness instead of truth and service to others, your foundation for living will be unreliable.

I knew a very ambitious man who lost sight of the fact that honoring personal relationships and following his values were more important than his personal desires. He became so focused on becoming president of his organization that his family suffered and all who worked with him suffered. He treated people with disrespect and mistook kindness for weakness. He eventually reached his goal to be president, but he held that office for less than a year. During his blind drive to satisfy his ambition, he had ignored commonly accepted values, and his motive appeared to be completely self-centered. You cannot lead without having a strong value base or without having compassion for others. A house built upon the sand will not stand. Examine your motives, and stay true to your ethical values and your purpose in life.

Be sure your dream career is in concert with your life's purpose. We are advised in Scripture to be careful what we treasure, because our hearts are where our treasures are![3]

DON'T BE A VICTIM

Have you ever known people who go through life perceiving themselves as victims? They believe that life's circumstances control them, and they just can't get a break. About the only good thing they get out of life is sympathy from others, so they unconsciously continue to be victims seeking sympathy. Such behavior is unproductive, destructive, and wasteful.

Bad things will happen to good people, but it is not the circumstance that should control you. You must take control of the circumstance. If something at work doesn't go right, you should resist the temptation to blame others. It is far more powerful to ask yourself what you might have done to help cause the problem. It is even more powerful to ask the follow-up questions of what you could do to fix the problem and what you could do to prevent the problem from recurring. If you begin to look at situations as though you helped create them instead of looking for someone to blame, you will gain control over your circumstances. If you continue to blame others, you will continue to allow circumstances to control you.

When someone makes a constructive suggestion about your behavior, do you consider the possibility that you need to modify that behavior, or do you dismiss it as jealous carping or whining by the other person? I suggest that it is far more powerful to be open to criticism and to consider what you might be able to change that will improve yourself. Even if the criticism is made in anger, it deserves healthy consideration. Are you able to apologize to others? Some people think it is a sign of weakness to apologize. It is really a sign of strength and maturity. Only insecure and prideful people have trouble apologizing. Now I ask you the big question: Can you forgive others for past wrongs?

Forgiving others is most difficult because our emotions and

our self-esteem are involved. Forgiving others has been a topic of interest to mankind since the beginning of time. In biblical times the apostle Peter asked Jesus how many times he should forgive another. The reply was seventy times seven times, or as often as you need to.[4] Jesus knew that holding a grudge adversely affects the person holding it. He also commanded that we love others as ourselves,[5] and that is not possible if you are nurturing some hurt done to you by another person. When someone betrays you or hurts you in some way, pray for him, forgive him, and begin thinking about more constructive things.

Forgiving others is also reciprocal. As you forgive someone for an infraction, you will experience immediate relief. If you think about all the mental energy and emotional stress involved in carrying a grudge, doesn't it make sense to let go? Think about each grudge as a weapon you're carrying around just waiting for a time to even the score. After a while all those weapons get pretty heavy, and besides, most of the people you are fretting about are no longer thinking about you. You are hurting only yourself when you nurse a grudge of some kind. Pray about it, forgive them, and move on. You will be a much happier and healthier person when you learn to forgive people.

BELIEVE

Many books have been written about the power of faith and belief. Claude Bristol studied world religions, cults, ancient magic, yoga, mental science, and many other effects of the mind. In his book *The Magic of Believing,* he states that many of the phenomena he studied were nonsense, others were strange, and some were profound. But "there was a golden thread that runs through all the teachings and makes them work for those who sincerely accept and apply them, and that thread can be named in a single word—*belief.*"[6] The element of belief has allowed some people to be healed, others to climb the ladder to great success, and still others to walk on hot coals. The ability to really believe something causes it to occur.

I took a freshman acting class in college, and I learned more about acting in one illuminating minute than I had learned all through high school and from acting in two class plays. It was a startling moment when I first read the words of the title of the college textbook. The title was *Acting Is Believing.* At first glance that title seems simple enough, but it profoundly affected me as I grasped the concept. The best actors have learned to believe they are the characters they play. Acting is believing, if only for the duration of the play or film. I don't remember another word or idea in that textbook, but I remember the most important words and that most profound concept after forty years.

Once you set your career goal, you have to believe you will get it. Believe it, execute your plan to get it, and you will have it at some point. If you don't really believe you can obtain your goal, throw in the towel or change your belief. I talked with a very talented gentleman the other evening who is serving as the interim president of an organization on whose board I sit. I asked him if he was going to apply for the permanent position. His reply was, "Yes, I am, but if I don't get it, I will be okay." He doesn't yet believe he can be selected for the job. I suggested he begin answering the question by stopping after the first three words of his response and begin believing that he is the best person for the job. I then told him I thought he would be perfect for the job. I hope that the power of suggestion will germinate into a more confident belief in himself.

WORDS HAVE MEANING

A brilliant federal judge was once asked to describe his philosophy of the judicial system. His reply? "Words have meaning." Words not only have meaning; they have power. Words stir people's hearts, inspire creativity, and even convict us. We could not think without words that connote meaning to concepts and ideas. We use words to provide self-talk to our inner man. We use words to encourage others, and they are encouraged. We can think and use words to encourage ourselves, and we are encouraged.

Words, like thoughts, manifest themselves into action. Words are reciprocal in nature. What you say comes back to you. If you say you are going to double your income by such and such a date, believe it, work toward that goal, and you will achieve it. If you say you just can't make it on your lousy salary, you will be setting a self-fulfilling prophecy. When you make a mistake, analyze it and learn from it, but don't whip yourself with mental or spoken words. Resolve to avoid the same mistake in the future, and recognize that you have just gained valuable experience to help you reach your next career goal. Keep your words positive, especially when speaking about your life and your career!

As you set your next career goal in your plan to get the career of your dreams, believe you will get it; then talk to yourself and others about it. Tell yourself you will achieve the promotion or get the next job by a certain date. Be specific: "I will have my CPA and be working for a big six accounting firm by June 1 of next year." Tell others about your goal. They will want to help you, and they will begin thinking about you in that job. Now you have not only yourself, but also others thinking positively and talking positively about you and the job you are seeking. This is great synergy, and sooner or later, probably on or before your target date, you will have the job, or one just like it.

Early in my career, I was advised not to tell other employees about my career plans because others could then attempt to sabotage them. I quickly realized that defensive thinking would not work for me. In my early twenties, I took the risk that my friends might laugh at me when I told them I intended to be a college president. They didn't laugh. In fact, they encouraged me. Even though it was a stretch for me to believe I could become a president, the more I talked about it, the more I believed it. Eventually I saw myself as a president and later became one.

DON'T GIVE UP

Winston Churchill is reputed to have given the shortest commencement address in history when he rose to the lectern and said, "Never give in. Never give in. Never, never, never, never." That was great advice more than sixty years ago, and it's sound advice today. Now that you understand the law of reciprocity, you know that all things sent will be returned in kind. We don't always have control of the timing, but we do know that to all things there is a season.

What if George Washington and his troops had given up? We probably would not have established the greatest republic the world has ever known. Tenacity and perseverance are two of the most important attributes you can have. As you learn patience and persistence, you achieve your goals. Stay focused, continue believing in yourself and your career vision, and keep working your plan. Stay too busy winning to lose. You will succeed!

SOME PARTING THOUGHTS ON RECIPROCITY

Life is all about choices, and your condition in life is pretty much a reflection of those choices. The great news is that with a little discipline and a clear vision for what you want to become, you can change your condition by thinking differently and making different choices. Your vision and your values should guide your thoughts, words, and deeds as you pursue your career dream. Expect change and adversity, but face these things with optimism and recognize them as opportunities to gain valuable experience. Continue setting higher career goals, and continue challenging yourself to grow in your career. Broaden your sphere of influence, and remember to give value first and treat people the way you want to be treated.

As you become a supervisor, remember the rule of reciprocity, and treat your subordinates with care, trust, and respect. Review their work in the broad context. It is unfair to point out their mistakes while ignoring their successes.

I recently held a governing board retreat where we discussed the major goals of the college and the strategies for achieving them. In one session, a staff member presented our college's results on the required state performance measures. We were thrilled to report that we achieved ten of the twelve measures, earning us a "superior" status and receiving a $100,000 award. To our surprise, several board members focused only on the two measures we had barely missed achieving, and their point of concentration affected staff morale. Of course, I have already determined how to present this data differently in the future so the focus will be more positive. We need to seek perfection, but I also need my staff members to feel good about themselves so they will continue to achieve superior results.

Your subordinates will want to repay you for your support. Give them opportunities to pay you back by achieving the goals you and your organization have established. This sets up another reciprocal opportunity, because success gives people confidence to achieve greater successes. Talk to your employees. Make sure they understand your vision and expectations and have the necessary information to make good decisions. When you talk with your staff, get to know them as individuals. Make sure you care about them. Don't just tell them you care about them; show them you care about them. Make your support of them greater than what they expect or what you expect in return. In fact, don't even think about what you will get out of the positive relationships with your staff. Just praise them for their achievements, and help them when they need to be helped. In short, treat your subordinates the way you want to be treated, and capitalize on the reciprocal benefits all the way to your dream job.

Remember, the best career vision, the most thorough preparation, and the best thinking and knowledge of how to be influential and capitalize on the power of reciprocity won't help a bit unless you execute your plan. Put your plan into action, and keep it in play until you achieve the career of your dreams. Of course, you should then start dreaming about a greater career!

| LADDER-BUILDING TIPS |

1. We are subject to the physical and spiritual laws of our universe.
2. We will prosper and achieve our goals by using these laws appropriately.
3. We must plant and cultivate for results.
4. Stay grounded in your broader life's purpose.
5. Stay focused and in control of your circumstances.
6. Learn to believe!
7. Words have meaning, and choices have consequences.

| LADDER-BUILDING ACTIONS |

1. I will take advantage of the power of reciprocity by

_____

_____

2. I will treat others as

_____

_____

3. I will avoid a victim's mentality by

_____

_____

4. The next steps toward achieving my career vision include

_____

_____

5. I will achieve these steps by the following dates:

_____

_____

| 7 |

LEADERSHIP AND ADVICE FROM THE PROS
Listen and Learn

Many receive advice, only the wise profit by it.
—Publius Syrus

The purpose of this brief bonus chapter is to provide a discussion of fifteen principles of leadership for those of you who aspire to be leaders or CEOs in your field. At the end of the chapter, every reader will benefit from the wonderful experiences of professionals who have achieved their dream careers.

LEARN TO LEAD

To gain the most gratification from your career and to provide the most influence for good, you must develop and use your leadership abilities. People who learn to accomplish goals through others are the people who get promotions and end up leading their organizations. Good leaders are able to influence others to accomplish a desired goal.

If your career goal includes becoming a good leader, you must realize that learning to lead is a never-ending quest. When you quit learning, you will cease to be an effective leader. Leading is not a thing to be achieved; it is a way of life. Leaders are constantly growing spiritually, mentally, and emotionally. They review the foundations of their character and endeavor to strengthen them every day. They know that true leadership comes from within them. Good leaders also review the basic principles of leadership and endeavor to use them more effectively.

I coauthored a book on leadership and concluded that most of the principles of leadership are fairly simple. But being simple does not necessarily mean they are easy to master.[1] All good leaders continue to improve these behaviors.

1. Commit to Excellence

People need to know that their leaders are committed before they will commit themselves. Committed leaders will demonstrate their commitment to their staff and their organizations on a consistent basis and in an unwavering manner.

2. Lead from a Personal Vision, Mission, and Set of Values

It is just as important to have a personal vision, mission, and set of values as it is for the organization to have its vision, mission, and set of values. A leader who has an unclear personal vision or set of values will soon have no one following. Great leaders know where they are going and have a solid set of values. They are anchored in truth, care about others, and believe in a moral authority.

3. Develop a Passion for the Job

The difference between good leaders and great leaders is not leadership style, charisma, or intelligence. Great leaders have a passion for what they do and whom they serve. Passion persuades people to follow you, and enthusiasm excites them to do their very best.

4. Build Trusting Relationships

People will not follow someone whom they distrust. Great leaders understand the importance of building and maintaining trusting relationships. If you have fragile or weak relationships with the people you are leading, your success at persuading, collaborating, and selling will be limited. Watch great leaders closely, and you will see that all of them concentrate on building relationships. They do this in two significant ways. When talking to someone, they concentrate on him as if he is the most important person in the room. They also ask for information about how things are going. They quickly try to develop some commonality with the other person to achieve rapport.

5. Lead for Results

Popular leaders are appreciated, but great leaders do more than create good relationships with their staff. Great leaders work with their team to accomplish great things. They have the ability to get things done.

6. Be Honest

Dishonesty ruins more careers than any other character flaw. Once your integrity is in question, the end is in sight. Successful leaders understand that it is far more important to tell the whole truth, even when it hurts, than to lie to others and shame themselves. Honest leaders are in high demand, especially since the Enron and Arthur Andersen debacles.

7. Be Fair and Respectful

People the world over have a keen sense of fairness, and they will be quick to perceive unfairness. Smart leaders recognize the importance and the ethics of treating all people with fairness and respect. Employees who perceive an inequity or disrespect from their leaders will and should rebel.

8. Be Humble

Confidence is a critical and compelling element for leaders, but so is humility. No one likes working with someone who claims all the glory and struts around with a superior attitude. Effective leaders see everyone as being just as important as themselves. They also remind themselves that they usually serve at the pleasure of someone else.

9. Be Optimistic

Nothing inspires people to excel more than a leader who has confidence in them. Even in the darkest of times, leaders must be optimistic and communicate a positive attitude to their subordinates. Overcautious leaders seldom achieve much.

10. Be a Good Communicator

If you can't encourage well or give clear directions, you won't be an effective leader. Successful leaders are good communicators in one-to-one conversations and in group settings. Great leaders have to be charismatic spokespersons for their team.

11. Be Adaptable

Successful leaders understand how to anticipate change and adapt to it. The mighty oak tree stands firm in the storm and breaks while the willow bends with the wind and remains. Change is part of life. Be a willow.

12. Know Your Business

Smart leaders have learned what they need to know in order to lead. These leaders not only know their field very well, but they have studied and learned the art of leadership. Smart leaders also seek new knowledge and skills in their field and in the business of leading people.

13. Delegate, but Verify

Effective leaders know that their employees make them and their organization successful or unsuccessful. No leader tries to do everything by himself, so he or she must learn to delegate. Although great leaders don't tell employees how to accomplish things, they do exercise judicious follow-through to ensure that the tasks have been properly accomplished.

14. Sweat the Small Stuff

Smart leaders understand that it is often the small things that disrupt progress. A vendor isn't paid on time, telephone calls aren't returned, a funeral is missed, or a paycheck is short—all may seem small to you, but they are big to those who are affected.

15. Accept Criticism; Share the Glory

Secure leaders learn to accept criticism and use it constructively. They also learn to credit their team for its accomplishments, and they learn to celebrate accordingly and often.

Astute leaders choose to follow a set of moral values, learn the self-discipline to apply them, and strive to lead by example. They also strive to be fair and trust their subordinates to achieve great things. They make informed choices and follow their instincts in making decisions that affect the integrity, quality, and image of their organization. They learn how to anticipate change and adjust to be successful in dealing with change. They learn how to negotiate so that both parties win. In the end, inspired leadership is about achieving common goals through others in a humble and collegial fashion. These final thoughts should be helpful as you learn to become more influential by leading:

- Make friends.
- Never make an enemy.
- Be yourself.
- Maintain integrity.
- Be confident.
- Be humble.
- Be optimistic.
- Have fun.[2]

GOOD ADVICE FOR GREAT CAREERS

I asked each of the following successful people the same question: "What advice would you give people who aspire to have successful careers?"

Some of these fine people are relatively young, most are in their fifties or sixties, and some are octogenarians. They represent both sexes and a diversity of ethnicities. I found their responses to be thoughtful, sometimes astounding, and always sincere. Each person believes in his or her advice. In fact, they have come to believe that their success is attributable to the same advice they are giving you. Their advice is powerful!

There is no perfect path to success. People become successful by working toward their dreams and by believing in them. In any event, you can learn valuable tips for getting a successful career by reading their advice and processing it for your use.

Continue learning throughout your career. Follow your passion, not your pension. Don't rely on your parents for career advice because the jobs of today are not the jobs of yesterday.

—Emily Stover DeRocco
Assistant Secretary for Employment and
Training, U.S. Department of Labor

Work hard and have good integrity. Be loyal to your employer and your customers. Demonstrate how your work contributes to the economic health of the company, and you won't have to worry about job security.

—John Belk
Chairman of the Board, Belk Stores Services, Inc.

Develop and use the qualities of integrity, dependability, optimism, competence, enthusiasm, commitment, hard work, and teamwork. Also, share your knowledge and enthusiasm to help others grow. Those who move ahead do so because they develop and teach others.

—Zig Ziglar
Chairman of the Board, Zig Ziglar Corp.

Carefully find an area in the company or business that you are just wild about and then go to work passionately! Bring new ideas to the workplace and be creative. Focus on gaining knowledge and personal growth.

—Allen Tate
CEO, Allen Tate Company

You will never have all the answers, so it is crucial to listen to and learn from those with whom you work. You also need to be willing to take advantage of new and unexpected opportunities, for each is an avenue for growth and exploration. But above all else, stay true to your convictions and follow the inner vision you have for your future.

—Krista Tillman
North Carolina CEO, Bell South

People the world over perform well at the workplace and develop organizational loyalty from being treated well, trusted, and encouraged to grow professionally. Remember to treat others well, trust them, and encourage them to grow professionally.

—Ambassador Mark Erwin
CEO, Erwin Capital
Former Ambassador to Mauritius

You have to make it happen. Get right with God, and then work hard.

—Joe Drury
CEO, Bojangles

Resolve to be the most positive and enthusiastic employee in your division or department. Strive to be the model for developing customer loyalty, and you will be greatly valued.

—Jim Bavis
Bavis Consulting

Work hard and be honest. Represent your company in a professional manner at all times, and be open to seeking new opportunities and challenges.

—Dale F. Halton
CEO, Pepsi-Cola Bottling, Charlotte

Find something you are passionate about.

—Ralph Pitts
General Counsel, Belk Stores Services, Inc.

The first step a person can take to have a great career is to attend college and make good grades. Study to acquire knowledge, not just to pass the course. Establish good relationships with your professors, and they will open doors for you. Get involved in campus activities, and take on leadership roles whenever possible.

—Hilda Gurdian
Co-owner, *La Noticia*, Charlotte

Do more than is expected of you.

—Mark Ethridge
Sports Publishing

Always be customer focused. Demonstrate early on your level of commitment to the company. Seek out ways to expand your knowledge base. Show flexibility and adaptability. Focus on how you can serve the company and make it better. Manage your career and be aggressive in a professional manner.

—Jane Cooper
Former CEO, Paramount Parks

Build a strong work ethic in your character, take charge of your health both physically and spiritually, and become competent in the product or service you provide. Seek balance in your life, and always give more than 100 percent.

—Al Allison
CEO, Allison Fence Company

Treat everyone with respect. Work hard, be harmonious, build trusting relationships, be a team player, and listen well. Finally, be positive and do your job the best you can, be dependable, and do what you say you will do.

—Jerry Richardson
Owner/Founder, Carolina Panthers

Never underestimate the importance of people skills. Intelligence and common sense are critical ingredients for performing and managing, but relationship skills are even more critical for leading.

—Jim Morgan
Former CEO, Interstate/Johnson Lane

To fully envision a future for yourself, write an essay of how your life will be when you become who you want to be. Include a reference to your company and how you will interact with it. Also describe your family life and personal life, then share this essay with everyone involved, including your boss. This will help to turn your life's plan into reality.

—Katie Tyler
President, Tyler 2 Construction

Surround yourself with good people.

—Rick Hendrick
CEO, Hendrick Motorsports

Learn to work with people.

—Darrell Holland
President, Pepsi-Cola Bottling, Charlotte

Set goals, be patient, but be persistent. Have a desire to win, and keep a positive attitude.

—Graham Keith
Chairman, The Keith Corporation

Be the first at work and the last to leave. Always help your fellow man. Read and try to follow the commands of Matthew 25:34–36.

—Tom Dooley
Founder, Dooley Construction

To get a successful career, remember that it is all about integrity.

—Peter Gilchrist
District Attorney
Mecklenburg County, North Carolina

Develop personal discipline. If you can't lead yourself, you can't lead others.

—Pete Sloan
Former CEO, Board Chair, Lance, Inc.

Be certain of your career choice in the first place.

—Larry Dagenhart
Attorney, Helms, Mulliss & Wicker

Hire people who are smarter than you.

—Tim Belk
CEO, Belk Stores Services, Inc.

Be positive, have a good attitude, and work hard, but don't become a workaholic. Spend time with your family.

—Phil Kirk
President, North Carolina Citizens for
Business and Industry

Demonstrate the ability to perform the job in the next level of the hierarchy, and learn jobs related to your immediate sphere of responsibility.

—Bill Dowdell
Former President,
Flexographic Technical Association

Continuously work on your character, your skills, your trustworthiness, your listening ability, and your ability to communicate at all levels.

—Frank Harrison
CEO, Coca-Cola Bottling, Charlotte

Do your job with enthusiasm and a positive attitude. Always learn as much as possible about your job and your career.

—Tony Fortino
Fortino Enterprises

Finding one's passion in life and then living it to its fullest is the one essential element, above all, for success.

—Tommy Norman
President, Norcom Properties

Decide to do only what you have an enormous passion for doing!

—Barry Weitz
Film Producer

Be customer focused and work to become indispensable to your employer. Become a lifelong learner and a teacher. Associate with people who can help you grow. When given responsibility, take charge. There is something important going on all the time. Look for it. Whatever your job, regardless of how menial it may appear at the time, do more than is required.

—James H. Amos Jr.
Chairman Emeritus, MBE/The UPS Store
Chairman & CEO, Sona MedSpa International

Read! Study successful managers and nurture a positive attitude. Take calculated risks, get involved, and go the extra mile every day. Honor your commitments.

—Ron Harper
CEO & Cofounder, Harper Corporation

CHARACTERISTICS AND BEHAVIORS DESIRED BY EMPLOYERS

While conducting this career-related research, I asked business executives to list the characteristics and behaviors that they most valued in employees. The following list demonstrates the most preferred attributes:

Positive attitude	Focused
Enthusiasm	Gets along with others
Trustworthy	Perseveres
Ability to communicate	Fair
Self-motivated	Creative
Team worker	Willing to change
Integrity	Flexible
Knowledgeable	Compassionate

Hard worker	Dependable
Loyal	Teachable
Ambitious	Ethical

SOME PARTING THOUGHTS

Congratulations! If you apply the principles outlined in this book, you will dramatically increase your chances to build a solid career ladder and achieve your dreams. Don't limit yourself, don't let others limit you, and don't let circumstances limit you. You were created to do great things, and by focusing on your unique abilities and capitalizing on the powers of vision, thought, influence, and reciprocity, you will be successful. Surround yourself with good people and people who can help you grow in your profession.

Forget about looking for job security. The only true job security rests with your belief in yourself, a clear career goal, a clear plan for success, and the discipline to work your plan. Once you recognize the truth of this matter, you will be free from the gripping fear of losing a job. By using the knowledge in this book, you will experience liberation from fear and any limitation that might bind you to an underemployment condition.

It will now be helpful if you will copy and review all of your responses to the Ladder-Building Actions that appeared at the end of each chapter. By putting these responses to paper, you will have designed a good basic plan for pursuing the career of your dreams. Look at it often. Adjust it as you need to, but follow it and stay focused on each goal along the way.

As you resolve to be enthusiastic and positive, obtain the right knowledge and workplace skills, and help others along the way, you will be sustained through the tough times and will ultimately achieve the success you desire.

You can begin now to face your next job or career move with confidence. You obviously have the personal motivation to excel at your career, or you would not have read this entire book in the first place. You can also have confidence that you have read the right book, know the universal secrets for gaining career success, and now have the opportunity to put your knowledge to work.

Believe me, you have the right stuff!

| LADDER-BUILDING TIPS |

1. Leaders learn to lead by studying and practicing leadership principles.
2. Wise people listen to and learn from people who have already achieved career success.

| LADDER-BUILDING ACTIONS |

1. Starting today, I will begin observing leaders to determine what makes them successful. I will especially observe

_____

_____

2. I will approach _____ and _____ for mentoring assistance.
3. I will reread the advice from the pros every _____.

NOTES

Chapter 1

1. Cam Report, "Career Advancement Management Facts and Trends," Priam Publications (East Lansing, MI), January 15, 2004.
2. Paul Kaihla, "The Coming Job Boom," *Business 2.0,* September 2003, 97–104.
3. Tony Zeiss, *The 12 Essential Laws for Getting a Job . . . and Becoming Indispensable* (Nashville: Thomas Nelson Publishers, 1997).

Chapter 2

1. Proverbs 29:18 KJV.
2. Joel Arthur Barker, Facilitator's Guide to *The Power of Vision,* the Video Series Discovery of the Future (Burnsville, MN: Chart House International Learning Corporation, 1993), 13.
3. Dr. Suess, *Oh, the Places You'll Go!* (New York: Random House, 1990).
4. Viktor Frankl, *Man's Search for Meaning* (Boston: Beacon Press, 1959), 115.
5. Barker, Facilitator's Guide, 13.
6. Ken Blanchard and Jesse Stoner, *Full Steam Ahead! Unleash the Power of Vision in Your Company and Your Life* (San Francisco: Berrett-Koehler Publishers, 2003).
7. Robert Collier, *Riches Within Your Reach: The Law of the Higher Potential* (Tarrytown, NY: Robert Collier Publications, 1947), 16.
8. Zeiss, *The 12 Essential Laws for Getting a Job . . . and Becoming Indispensable.*
9. *Magill's Encyclopedia of Social Science: Psychology,* vol. 4 (Pasadena, California: Salem Press, 2003), 1700.
10. Jack Canfield and H. C. Wells, *100 Ways to Enhance Self-Concept in the Classroom* (Englewood Cliffs, New Jersey: Prentice Hall, 1976).
11. Claude Bristol, *The Magic of Believing* (New York: Pocket Books, 1969), 56.

Chapter 3

1. Proverbs 23:7.
2. Ronald Kotulak, *Inside the Brain* (Kansas City, MO: Andrews McMeel, 1997), 161.
3. Ibid., 165.
4. Ibid., 4.

5. Dr. Linda Elder and Dr. Richard Paul, *The Miniature Guide to Taking Charge of the Human Mind*, 3rd ed. (Dillon Beach, CA: Foundation for Critical Thinking, 2002).

6. James Zull, *The Art of Changing the Brain* (Sterling, VA: Stylus Publishing, 2002), 5.

7. Robert Collier, *The Book of Life* (Tarrytown, NY: Robert Collier Publications, 1925), 118–23.

8. Elder and Paul, *The Miniature Guide to Taking Charge of the Human Mind*, 21.

9. John C. Maxwell, *Thinking for a Change* (New York: Warner, 2003), 54.

Chapter 4

1. Dr. Wayne W. Dyer, *Staying on the Path* (Carlsbad, CA: Hay House, 1995), 93.

2. Frankl, *Man's Search for Meaning*, 115.

3. Brent Q. Hafen and others, *Mind/Body Health: The Effects of Attitudes, Emotions, and Relationships* (Needham Heights, MA: Allyn and Bacon, 1996), 2.

4. Hafen and others, *Mind/Body Health*, 89–92.

5. Dr. Herbert Benson, *The Relaxation Response* (William Morrow, 1975; New York: Harper Torch, 2000).

6. Hafen and others, *Mind/Body Health*, 386–94.

7. Proverbs 17:22.

8. Hafen and others, *Mind/Body Health*, 547.

9. James Allen, *The Wisdom of James Allen* (San Diego: Laurel Creek Press, 2001), 41.

10. Allen, *The Wisdom of James Allen*, 16.

11. Dyer, *Staying on the Path*, 299.

12. Rick Warren, *The Purpose-Driven Life* (Grand Rapids: Zondervan, 2002), 17.

13. Allen, *The Wisdom of James Allen*, 45.

14. Elder and Paul, *The Miniature Guide to Taking Charge of the Human Mind*, 21.

15. Ibid., 24–25.

16. Allen, *The Wisdom of James Allen*, 85.

17. Justin Martin, "Practical Dreamer," *Fortune Small Business,* December 2004–January 2005, 43–50.

18. Ellyn Spragins, "Thought Power," *Fortune Small Business,* December 2004–January 2005, 52.

19. Bristol, *The Magic of Believing,* 44–45.

20. Collier, *The Book of Life*, 237.

21. Bristol, *The Magic of Believing*, 42.
22. Collier, *The Book of Life*, 98.

Chapter 5

1. Bristol, *The Magic of Believing*, 106.
2. Zig Ziglar, *Ziglar on Selling* (New York: Ballantine, 1991), 29.
3. Truett Cathy, *It's Easier to Succeed Than to Fail* (Nashville: Thomas Nelson Publishers, 1989), 47.
4. John Spencer and Karen Shanor, "Mind-Body Medicine," in *The Emerging Mind* (Los Angeles: Renaissance Books, 1999), 137.
5. Tony Zeiss, *Nine Essential Laws for Becoming Influential* (Tulsa: Triumphant Publishers, International, 2000).
6. Psalm 118:24.
7. Brent Q. Hafen and others, "Self-Esteem and Health," in *Mind/Body Health*, 486.

Chapter 6

1. 2 Corinthians 9:6.
2. Collier, *Riches Within Your Reach*, 107.
3. Matthew 6:21.
4. Matthew 18:21–22.
5. Mark 12:31.
6. Bristol, *The Magic of Believing*, 4–5.

Chapter 7

1. Gunder Myran, George A. Baker III, Beverly Simone, and Tony Zeiss, *Leadership Strategies for Community College Executives* (DC: Community College Press, 2003), 122–23. Tony Zeiss, author of the chapter "First Year Strategies for New Presidents."
2. Ibid., 132–33.

ABOUT THE AUTHOR

Dr. Tony Zeiss serves as president of Central Piedmont Community College, the largest college in North Carolina, with seventy thousand students. Zeiss has authored or coauthored several books on economic development, adult literacy, and national workforce development. Zeiss holds a doctorate in community college administration, a master's degree in speech (radio and television), and a bachelor's degree in speech education. He is a committed Christian and family man.

Dr. Zeiss is also a professional speaker and a member of the National Speakers Association. He is a frequent keynoter for companies and colleges on recruiting, developing, and retaining peak performers at the workplace. He regularly consults with states and regions on economic development. Zeiss is past chair of the board of the American Association of Community Colleges and past board chair of The League for Innovation. He was the Association of Community College Trustees' National CEO of the year for 2004-05. He serves on several local, regional, and national boards and frequently serves as a workgroup participant for the U. S. Department of Education and the U. S. Department of Labor.

ACKNOWLEDGMENTS

I wish to thank all of the wonderful people who rendered assistance with this book, especially my assistant, Susan Oleson, and a most resourceful librarian, Ann Shearer. I also wish to thank my wife, Beth, who for twenty-seven years has unselfishly supported my career and my writing while working as a full-time educator and mother.

I am grateful to be able to work with Nelson Business, a division of Thomas Nelson Publishers; Victor Oliver; and my editor, Kristen Parrish.

Finally, I wish to thank my father, Robert E. Zeiss, and my mother, Mary A. Zeiss, for sowing the seeds of this book in my mind many years ago.

──── Also by Dr. Tony Zeiss ────

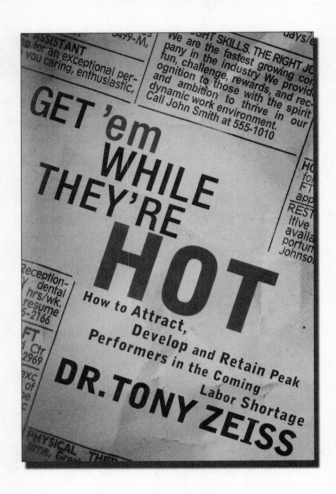

NELSON BUSINESS
A Division of Thomas Nelson Publishers
Since 1798

www.thomasnelson.com